# The Transformation Curve to World-Class

# The Transformation Curve to World-Class

Steven Leuschel
from Interviews with Rodger Lewis

Align Kaizen Publishing
Ridgway, PA

© 2022 Align Kaizen Publishing

All rights reserved. No part of this book may be reproduced without written permission from the publisher, except by a reviewer who may quote brief passages in a review; nor may any part of this book be stored in a retrieval system, or transmitted in any form or by any means—electronic, mechanical, photocopying, recording, or other—without written permission from the publisher.

Published by Align Kaizen Publishing
Indiana, PA

ISBN13: 978-0-9991897-7-1

Project coordination by Jenkins Group, Inc.
www.jenkinsgroupinc.com

Printed in the United States of America
26 25 24 23 22 • 5 4 3 2 1

# Contents

FOREWORD
   by Bettina Baumgartner — vii

PREFACE
   My Understanding of the Transformation Curve
      by Steven Leuschel — ix

INTRODUCTION
   Learning and Adapting the Curve
      by Rodger B. Lewis — xiii

CHAPTER 1
   Creating the Transformation Curve from Toyota's Culture — 1

CHAPTER 2
   Phase One Tools for Top-Level Engagement — 13

CHAPTER 3
   Continuous Improvement Training and Implementation — 37

CHAPTER 4
   The Pilot Area—Coaching and Tools — 55

CHAPTER 5
   Expanding Phase One with an Organizational Strategy — 75

CHAPTER 6
   Sustaining Continuous Improvement through Audits — 85

CHAPTER 7
   Phase Two, Level C — 95

# Foreword

## by Bettina Baumgartner

I am fascinated by Lean culture and Lean transformation. This started more than 20 years ago when I was asked to be part of a Lean transformation in a brown field implementation. Rodger Lewis had just transitioned from General Motors to BRP Rotax.

At the time, I was unaware of how little I really knew about Operational Excellence, Lean, Transformation, etc. despite everything I already had read and learned. Since I was introduced to the Transformation Curve and the Journey to World-Class from Rodger, I have become a life-long learner.

I have been working, struggling, and loving the subject of Lean in many different ways: a change agent, trainer, production leader, PhD-researcher, and executive. Over this time, especially during my doctoral dissertation years, I have read countless books about Lean, Toyota, and culture. So why should you, as a reader, be interested in yet another one?

I believe that Rodger Lewis is one of the few people who have a deep insight not only into Toyota's culture, but how to bring the culture alive in a pre-world class environment. Even if you have experienced the future-state at Toyota, it does not mean that you know how to develop and transform an organization into its own world class culture. Being a copycat of Toyota tools may lead to short-term success, but will be doomed to fail on the long run if the tools aren't aligned with the organization's desired culture.

Many organizations pursue tools and operation system effectiveness while neglecting culture. Based upon my doctoral research, it is not possible to reach beyond a certain level of production system effectiveness without specific culture tools and elements in place. As a result I proposed a culture model of effective production systems which explains the interrelation of cultural imperatives, differentiators and enablers.

Rodger is one of the rare individuals who have mastered both applied and comprehensive knowledge about the Toyota Production System and adapting it to brownfield organizations along his life-long learning journey.

Steven is attempting the challenging task of capturing the essence of this life-long journey, which cannot be applauded enough. Without his own experience in bringing Lean into healthcare and his consulting experience with Rodger, this would not be possible. Many professionals—Lean doers and thinkers—will be able to learn from, and build on, the brief description of the Lean Transformation Curve and the Lean journey described in this book.

If there is one key message that cannot be highlighted enough from this book, it is the insight to focus on the positive and to foster the positive during any transformation journey. I think to ignore this is one of the most dangerous, yet common mistakes in a Lean implementation journey.

So keep reading, keep learning, keep improving and keep hunting for the positive during your journey towards real Lean transformation!

# Preface

# My Understanding of the Transformation Curve

by Steven Leuschel

In my first book, *Lean Culture Change* (2015), I presented a theory on how and why organizations adopt the Toyota Production System (TPS). Many people and organizations initially experience Toyota in the form of kaizen (improvement) events and then tool implementation subsequent to those events. Furthermore, they experience TPS as developing leaders within Toyota, as suppliers to Toyota, or as individuals observing and writing about Toyota.

Throughout the last few decades of TPS adaptation and implementation across North America and the world, I've seen more and more organizations understand the *why* and *what* of TPS but very few that are able to grasp and articulate the *how* as it relates to complete organizational transformation. Even fewer leaders are able to repeat it.

Decades after the introduction of TPS into North America, even the best organizations that primarily started with kaizen events and "Lean" tools have come to realize that there's a better way. The majority of organizations and practitioners have been listening to the majority of leaders, consultants, and practitioners who have learned a great deal but whose starting point for Lean is very different from those of the early leaders of Toyota in North America. If we do not reflect back on the lessons these individuals can teach, we are destined to repeat mistakes (and waste time and money) that could readily be avoided.

Rodger Lewis has clearly demonstrated through his own actions and through learners of the Transformation Curve—a guide for changing organizations by teaching them how to sequence specific tools to perpetuate success—that the long-term approach has been successfully adapted and applied for decades globally, not just by him but by those very learners.

Along with many others, I believe the Transformation Curve is part of the fundamental countermeasure to the long-standing problem of North America's failed, stalled, or slow moving Lean implementation.

Thanks to Rodger, learners of the Transformation Curve directly or indirectly have been gaining traction over the last decade, demonstrating that there is a better way to "implement Lean" than just by events, doing Lean, or simply focusing on the needs of the organization without a long-term strategy to change. His experience at and after Toyota Georgetown was much different from many other early adopters of Lean and TPS.

While many thought leaders may still disagree that there can be a standard approach to changing organizations, these same thought leaders as well as Lean practitioners who preach that we must come up with one best way to change a particular process or standard often fail to recognize that organizational change is also a process. In fact, it's a long, complex process, but that shouldn't stop us from trying to understand a systematic, repeatable approach to transforming organizations.

Our conversations need to shift towards how to *build* the TPS house and become less focused on how to *apply* the house of TPS. Based on my knowledge of the curve and the current literature available, the Transformation Curve is simply the best way to build the adapted TPS house known to date. This book is consequently a high-level introduction to the Transformation Curve.

Of course, the Transformation Curve in no way guarantees perfection or even success in changing an organization. It does, however, provide a different context, starting point, and long-term, systematic, and repeatable plan. Individuals learning the Transformation Curve make mistakes, but their mistakes are in a far different context than the mistakes of those who do not have such a long-term plan. If you want to change an organization, if you want to be successful with Lean Transformation, you must have a plan and know how to check it. Having a plan that has been repeated globally in a multitude of industries is far superior to any one example of a theoretical plan or completely customized plan with no consideration of transformation standards.

I've been studying and applying the Transformation Curve for more than ten years as a student, consultant, internal coach, researcher, and writer. Each step in the journey has been a different learning experience, all rooted in the Transformation Curve. I know a fraction of what Rodger knows and a fraction of the Transformation Curve, but I have seen firsthand the success the long-term plan brings to leaders and organizations.

Rodger and I teamed up for this book because while many individuals believe in the Transformation Curve, it's nearly impossible to articulate a summary without overwhelming key decision makers. I interviews Rodger for this book so that individuals who believe in the curve and have seen it change an organization can communicate the plan to executives who can lead enterprise-wide change. This book is tainted with my own experiences and understanding of the curve and reflects merely a small piece of Rodger's understanding on how to change an organization.

When Rodger and I first met in 2005 at Saint Vincent College, the curve was essentially solidified, having been modified slightly from his late 1990's version. At that time, adapting the curve to organizations was a mixture of what we knew was right and the coaching clients would purchase and be willing to use.

As a center within Saint Vincent College, our team trained, coached, and adapted the Transformation Curve to meet the needs of clients. Rodger was the sensei, we were coaches of the curve—we were all simultaneously learning the curve and trying to sustain a business unit. Many executives and other leaders at that time (and still today) said that taking five years to fully implement the plan was far too long. Comments such as, "We don't have that much time; we need to change now," were common. This attitude led to organizations choosing short-term approaches and false promises of kaizen events, process reengineering, and other traditional TPS tool implementation. The results of this choice are obvious.

My hope is that the leaders and change agents of today and tomorrow can use this book to begin what I call the Journey to World Class, focusing on the positive and improving themselves, their organizations, and our communities together. In offering a high-level overview of the Transformation Curve, this book is a great starting point from which to begin, align, and reinvigorate your transformation journey. Enjoy!

# Introduction

# Learning and Adapting the Curve

by Rodger B. Lewis

My life has taken many twists and turns, from the Vietnam War to Saint Vincent College to Volkswagen, Toyota, and General Motors. At Saint Vincent, I learned the Benedictine Values and the importance of patience; this laid the groundwork for the Transformation Curve, or how to change organizations by teaching them how to sequence specific tools to perpetuate success.

My experiences at Volkswagen, Toyota, and General Motors occurred during a revolutionary time in the auto industry as the application of the Toyota Production System (TPS) began to infiltrate North America. I'm not smarter than anyone else, but where I began learning about TPS is vastly different from where most others begin.

Since my experiences at Toyota Georgetown, learning Toyota's culture from a very early point in Toyota's history in North America, my efforts to apply and modify TPS using the Transformation Curve have helped me transform organizations around the globe to live with mutual trust and respect while sustaining world-class results.

## Volkswagen

I've loved cars my entire life.

# The Transformation Curve to World-Class

In 1976, when I found out that Volkswagen was starting a plant in my hometown of Mount Pleasant, Pennsylvania, I decided to do whatever it took to work there. Thanks to my previous experience at Wilson Freight as a superintendent of transportation, I was hired into Volkswagen in the same role.

I helped prepare the new facility for production, prepared myself to help with the actual production of cars as my role shifted into production, and accompanied the president to Germany, where we studied how to build a car. For the first time, I built a car by myself, except for the body, piece by piece. I made my own instruction manual, standardizing the work, so that when I returned, I could teach others how to build cars.

Thanks to Volkswagen, I really thought I knew how to build a car. I was with the company for over ten years and never had a grievance from the union, so I felt like I knew labor relations and how to lead a workforce, too.

After I became the internal coordinator of quality overseeing quality parts within all of VW's companies, I also understood quality, or at least what quality should be.

Once I became the superintendent of production, I really thought I knew how to build a car—until I went to Toyota.

## Toyota Georgetown

In 1985 or 1986, one of the suppliers for both Volkswagen and Toyota contacted me and offered me a position. I really wasn't interested in leaving Volkswagen, and I especially didn't want to work for a supplier. I didn't realize then that Toyota was using its suppliers to recruit individuals for its Georgetown facility.

Around the same time I was contacted again, I found out my VW plant was closing and that I would be transferred to China, Wolfsburg, or somewhere else. More importantly, I also found out that the supplier job was actually with Toyota.

I loved cars so much and was so determined to learn more about them that I would have paid to work at Toyota. At the time, I had no idea that Toyota didn't just develop cars but also developed people. Once I learned this, I would use it for the rest of my life and teach it to others.

At Toyota, I became the manager of inspection and the manager of quality, and this was the true beginning of my journey.

I was the only American in the quality and engineering group with prior automotive experience. A few other Americans and I hired all the employees and helped with the layout and building of the plant, design of the product, development of the culture, and the ramp-up to full production.

In 1989, three years after I was hired, we launched the Toyota Georgetown plant. We built the best car in North America in 1990 and won the gold plant award from J.D. Power and Associates in 1991 and again in 1992. This was an experience like none other, and it provided me with much of the knowledge I used to design the Transformation Curve and help other organizations become world class from both an operations and human development perspective.

## General Motors

In 1994, I began applying the Toyota Production System inside the Opel Division of General Motors. At this point, I knew how the Japanese must have felt about me when I came on board, because now I was trying to change the culture and teach the Toyota Way to GM.

It was at this transition that I developed the first iteration of the Transformation Curve, a systematic sequenced approach to adapting and introducing TPS. I knew I couldn't just walk into GM with Toyota's version of standardized work, andon systems, culture, and so on and expect it to actually work. I wasn't just going to run kaizen events when we were up against a problem. I knew I had to sequence the tools and start out simply, developing the culture first.

The Opel plant in Germany was my first challenge, and within three years, we had a version of TPS up and running, including a pull system, andons, kanbans, team-based problem solving, team structure, one-piece flow, etc., all starting with culture.

After that, I was involved with establishing plants and the system in Poland, Argentina, Thailand, and China. At each of those plants, I used the Transformation Curve, brought in a leader from Toyota, and led the development of the system strategically by flying to each location at least once a month for several years using the Transformation Curve as my guide.

Having demonstrated that the curve would work outside of Toyota, I now wanted to adapt it further to work outside the auto industry.

## Beyond the Auto Industry

When I was approached by the Bombardier family to help at their facility in Austria, I made it very clear that the Transformation Curve was about safety, quality, and developing culture, not just finance.

In Austria, they called me the "Crazy American Cowboy" because I guaranteed everyone's job, I communicated the system to everyone, and I engaged everyone in the plan—the Transformation Curve. The people did all the work, but I taught, coached, and performed much-needed Plan-Do-Check-Act, or PDCA.

After five years, the results exceeded the world-class targets we had set in safety, quality, productivity, human development, cost, and operational excellence. Most importantly, we kept the headcount the same, just as I'd promised. None of it would have been possible without mutual trust and respect—i.e., the culture inherent within the Transformation Curve.

## Adapting the Transformation Curve

At that time, I came back to Saint Vincent and started teaching the system to learners such as Dick Hills, David Adams, Dr. Rick Kunkle, Allan Edwards, Steve Leuschel, and others. I also began expanding the system into the rest of Bombardier, both aerospace and transportation.

Under my coaching, learners at Saint Vincent adapted the system to the service industry as well as to manufacturing, paper/pulp, healthcare, and other industries. At Saint Vincent, we repeated the curve and saw that it works in virtually any industry with people and processes as long as the emphasis remains on culture, mutual trust, and respect.

The purpose of this book is to introduce the Transformation Curve to organizations that want to use it as their high-level plan in order to become world class. Lean tools are an essential part of the Transformation Curve, but without a long-term strategy and sequenced approach, the tools are only tools. Once they are sequenced and adapted to change culture, drive results, and align organizations, the result is world-class performance.

The Transformation Curve starts with culture first and sustains it throughout the generations of leadership, making it a sustainable system larger than any one individual or team. Today, the Transformation Curve has become a model for adapting the Toyota Way and the Toyota Production System to the auto, aerospace, manufacturing, service, and healthcare industries.

My hope for this book is to shift thinking towards complete organizational transformation rooted in the systematic, repeatable approach that is the Transformation Curve.

# Chapter 1

# Creating the Transformation Curve from Toyota's Culture

Traditionally, most companies in the global automobile industry shared similar cultures—think command and control—and many initial leaders at Toyota Georgetown brought that culture with them to Toyota, including Rodger Lewis, one of the first few leaders hired to Toyota Georgetown from Volkswagen in the 1980s.

This newly forming team of leaders at Georgetown quickly realized that the command and control way of managing people wouldn't work at Toyota. Instead, their own individual cultures and leadership styles needed to drastically change. To manage their behaviors, these leaders put together a system using nothing more than sticky notes, two per leader.

In Rodger's case, he wrote the words "Rodger's Culture" on one of his sticky notes. On the other, he wrote "Toyota's Culture."

Every day, Rodger would switch the "Rodger's Culture" and "Toyota's Culture" sticky notes before and after leaving the Georgetown plant. While in the plant, whenever he started reverting to his old behaviors, he would pull out his day planner and look at that little note, "Toyota's Culture." He would then relax and use the behaviors his senseis were teaching him and other leaders at Georgetown.

When he went home, he would put the "Toyota's Culture" sticky note in his glove box and pull out the "Rodger's Culture" note, because now he was ready to go out, drink beer, have a good time, and express "Rodger's Culture."

One day, while cleaning out his car, Rodger found the "Rodger's Culture" sticky note. He asked himself, "When did I quit changing notes? And when did I start carrying my Toyota culture into my daily life outside of Toyota?"

On Monday, he called his peers and asked if they still had their sticky notes.

None of them were using the sticky note system anymore. What's more, the Georgetown leaders realized that the culture of the entire plant had changed. As one, they wondered, "When did that happen?"

No one was arguing, no one was swearing, and no one was in anybody's face, all of which were daily occurrences in the U.S. auto industry. None of these negative behaviors existed any longer at Toyota Georgetown. The leaders realized they had changed their own culture, though they didn't know exactly when, and they started to wonder, "When did everybody else's culture change, too?"

## Adapting the Toyota Way

Most people get confused when adapting the Toyota Production System (TPS). They think it's about adapting tools to solve problems, and they don't understand the culture necessary to become and sustain world-class results. Many books and materials about TPS, Lean, and other Toyota ideas contain all the tools of TPS and how they might be perceived, observed, and experienced, everything from 5S to engineering to purchasing strategy, but they don't address the culture.

Many organizations try but most fail to implement TPS because they don't look at the difference between their own cultures and the Toyota Way. They don't understand how to sequence the tools and change the culture to support organization-wide transformation.

At Toyota, the culture is inherent. It's part of daily living. But because it's part of daily living, it's second nature. That's why it may be difficult for team members within Toyota to articulate what they are doing, let alone explain how to adapt and sequence the thinking to other organizations.

At Toyota, the tools don't have to be sequenced because they are already aligned, linked, and interconnected. People at Toyota don't have to realize, for example, that leadership must grasp the 5 Whys before introducing one-page reports. They don't have to grasp that an organization needs simple 5S working before introducing a pull system. At Toyota, they know how to build cars, support teamwork, and use the tools in the toolbox. In other words, they don't have to know how to transform an organization because they are already aiming at true north together every day.

## Why Sequencing Matters

When Rodger went to General Motors, he already knew the U.S. auto industry, thanks to his experiences at Volkswagen and Toyota. He knew he couldn't just take his "bag of Toyota goodies" to General Motors and expect to implement TPS. He couldn't just wait for a problem to occur, take a tool from his Toyota toolbox, and solve the problem. Moreover, he couldn't just hand everybody else the toolbox and say, "Learn what's in this toolbox, and when we need something, we'll pull it out."

Instead, he had to develop and test an approach to introduce and sustain TPS using less complex tools initially to drive the daily behaviors necessary to become world class. Thus, the first iteration of the Transformation Curve—a sequenced approach to introducing and adapting the Toyota Production System—began.

## The Transformation Curve

Complex tools must be sequenced in manageable pieces so that leaders and organizations can be successful and learn more complex tools. Cultural change doesn't happen by pointing out all the negatives and solving those problems. People must see and know success so that they can replicate it.

In terms of sequencing, many people think, "I can start with kaizen events" or "I'll just start with 5S." That's possible, but if leaders don't have a sequential understanding of the tools and how they interlink with each other, they won't be able to formulate a long-term strategy for change.

Rather than jumping into A3s, value stream mapping, and kaizen events, tokens of the Toyota Production System, leaders must grasp the long-term strategy inherent in the Transformation Curve, shown in Figure 1.1 on the next page.

# The Transformation Curve to World-Class

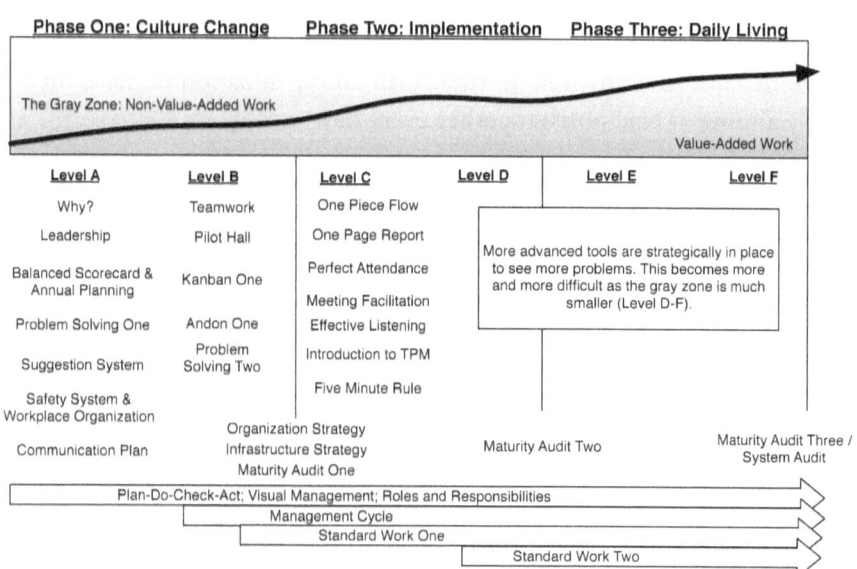

Figure 1.1

The "curve" has three phases: cultural change, implementation, and daily living. If an organization chooses to embark on this three-phase journey, 90% of the improvement portion is going to be in Phase One, cultural change, and parts of Phase Two, implementation. The remainder of Phase Two and all of Phase Three, daily living, is for organizations that have mastered Phase One and are managing and improving a very small gray zone with complex problems.

This book focuses on the specific tools of Phase One (Levels A and B) as well as Phase Two, Level C because the curve becomes more and more complex as different tools and strategies are introduced.

## *Phase One, Level A*

The initial tools of Phase One—understanding why, leadership, balanced scorecard, annual planning, communication plan, improvement system, safety system, workplace organization, and problem solving one—begin to create a framework to impact the behaviors needed to become world class.

**Understanding Why:** This tool facilitates an understanding of why the organization must change and the long-term strategy for change—the Transformation Curve and the Journey to World Class.

**Leadership:** This tool encompasses the behaviors, team, and commitment necessary from a leadership perspective to begin organizational transformation using the Transformation Curve.

**Balanced Scorecard and Annual Planning:** These tools establish organizational standards for setting long-term targets, interim targets, and well-formulated plans to achieve those targets.

**Communication Plan:** This is the plan for communicating to the organization's workforce and community the systematic approach, expectations of the journey, and commitment from leadership.

**Improvement System:** This is the first portion of the Continuous Improvement Program introduced in Chapter 3. In Level A, the suggestion or improvement system is focused on individual suggestions.

**Safety System and Workplace Organization:** These tools include organizational standards for safety and creating a safe, visual workplace.

**Problem Solving One:** This tool offers an introduction to the standards of problem solving integrated into the daily behaviors of the organization, including problem identification, root cause analysis, and creating, implementing, and checking countermeasures.

In terms of sequencing, some of these Level A tools are applied to the leadership team first, primarily balanced scorecard, annual planning, and problem solving one. This is discussed further in Chapter 2.

Level A tools that are introduced later, including the improvement system, safety system, and workplace organization, are introduced in the pilot hall or the entire organization (depending on the plan). All the tools of Phase One are applied in this general order as on the curve into the pilot, which helps leaders link frontline processes with the strategic plan.

*PHASE ONE, LEVEL B*

The later tools of Phase One prepare the organization for further adaptation and implementation of TPS to achieve results. They include selecting a pilot hall, establishing teamwork, and using simple kanban and andon. More complex problem solving known as problem solving two is also introduced in Level B. The tools of Phase One, Level B are primarily introduced in the pilot hall and linked with the executive team. They are discussed further in Chapter 4 but are briefly defined below.

**Teamwork:** This includes team suggestions (an aspect of the Continuous Improvement Program), team structure, and cultural standards for supporting one another within a team and other teams in the organization.

**Pilot Hall:** This is a frontline area to test the tools of the Transformation Curve and show the organization what it will look like in, for example, five years. The pilot hall appears in both the Transformation Curve and the Journey to World Class to help visually link the two models even further.

**Kanban One:** This is an introduction to an internal material management system that reduces inventory, increases floor space, and establishes clear signals and standards for replenishment.

**Andon One:** This is an introduction to linking standards, processes, and team structure with a help chain so the organization and team knows very clearly who needs to respond when. Its purpose is proactive problem solving.

**Problem Solving Two:** This is more complex problem solving that integrates problem solving one and teamwork to solve more complex problems; it links back to the overall system.

These tools are introduced after Level A because they are not functional or sustainable without Level A in place. They are introduced to the pilot hall first rather than throughout the entire organization because the tools must be all interlinked and aligned with the executive team's transformation. For example, implementing kanban one without an understanding of workplace organization would be unsustainable. To introduce andons without team structure and problem solving one in place at both the pilot and executive levels would not result in proactive problem solving supported with top-down coaching. In other words, Level B begins to prompt the question, "How do I support the teams above, below, and side to side of mine?" It also includes using the management cycle on a daily basis to link the tools to results, which not only supports the behaviors but also links world-class behaviors with world-class results.

*Transitioning from Phase One to Phase Two*

Organizationally, there must be enough teams or pilot areas in Phase Two to support the transition of the entire organization from Phase One to Phase

Two. This transition includes organizational strategy, infrastructure strategy, and maturity audit one. The general concept of each is explained below.

**Organizational Strategy:** This ensures that the right team and organizational structure is in place to support world-class team behaviors linked to results. It connects the overall compensation strategy of the organization with results to further support teamwork throughout the enterprise.

**Infrastructure Strategy:** This aligns the operations, square footage, and processes with the organizational strategy.

**Maturity Audit One:** This is a cultural check to ensure that Phase One tools are functional and improving per the plan.

This book covers organizational strategy and why it is necessary for the executive leader and the executive team to grasp the long-term approach to creating this strategy. The leader must not only commit to a social pact but must understand the plan necessary to fulfill it. Infrastructure strategy is not covered in this book due to the detail necessary to explain it as well as the number of existing books that cover this subject.

## PHASE TWO, LEVEL C

This phase includes tools to drive results and sustain the cultural behaviors and processes introduced in Phase One. The tools in this phase are briefly introduced below.

**One-Piece Flow:** This is a strategy for products, services, supplies, etc. to move one at a time from a push system to a pull or flow system.

**One-Page Report:** This is a communication standard to summarize and fit information to one page, initially to summarize balanced scorecards, master plans, problem solving, and continuous improvement activities. This tool, also called A3, is used in Phases Two and Three of the Transformation Curve.

**Perfect Attendance:** This is a program to increase engagement, positive recognition, and attendance.

**Meeting Facilitation:** This includes standards for planning, executing, facilitating, and checking meetings. Kaizen—continuous improvement—events are introduced as a subcomponent of meeting facilitation.

**Effective Listening:** This mechanism for grasping information quickly is linked to meeting facilitation and one-page reports; it aids understanding and the ability to make decisions efficiently and effectively.

**Introduction to Total Preventative Maintenance (TPM):** This introduction to TPM establishes standards to proactively maintain processes, system standards, and the general workplace flow and organization.

**Five-Minute Rule:** This standard links the tools of Phase One and Phase Two. Essentially, it means that anything from a balanced scorecard to a master plan to a one-page report to standard work must be understood within five minutes to ensure that problems can be solved very quickly.

## The Journey to World Class

Because organizations are multidimensional, it's not enough to simply take the Transformation Curve and apply all the tools in a linear fashion. The sequenced approach to the tools must be overlapped with the steps required to become world class. The tools cannot be implemented everywhere all at once due to organizational and personal capacity constraints. If time and resources were endless, this might be possible, but that isn't the case in most organizations. This is why top-level engagement, a plan to apply continuous improvement, a pilot area, and a plan to extend and sustain implementation are all necessary.

Grasping this and implementing these tools step by step makes it possible to understand the cycle of adoption, implementation, and diffusion of different tools to build a comprehensive system and culture in the organization. This Journey to World Class is summarized in Figure 1.2.

Overlapping the Journey to World Class with the Transformation Curve gives guidance on which tools to apply and when and must be adapted and planned depending on the current state of each organization.

### Grasping the Business Case

The Journey to World Class starts with a sensei—a teacher—doing his or her due diligence through "go and sees," getting the facts, and genuinely understanding what and where the organization is today. Most organizations have non-standard processes, services, and products. In most organizations, the culture, process, delivery services, and products are not aligned to world-class standards. On the other hand, if leaders learn how to lead people and manage processes, they can generally apply TPS to their organizations to transform them.

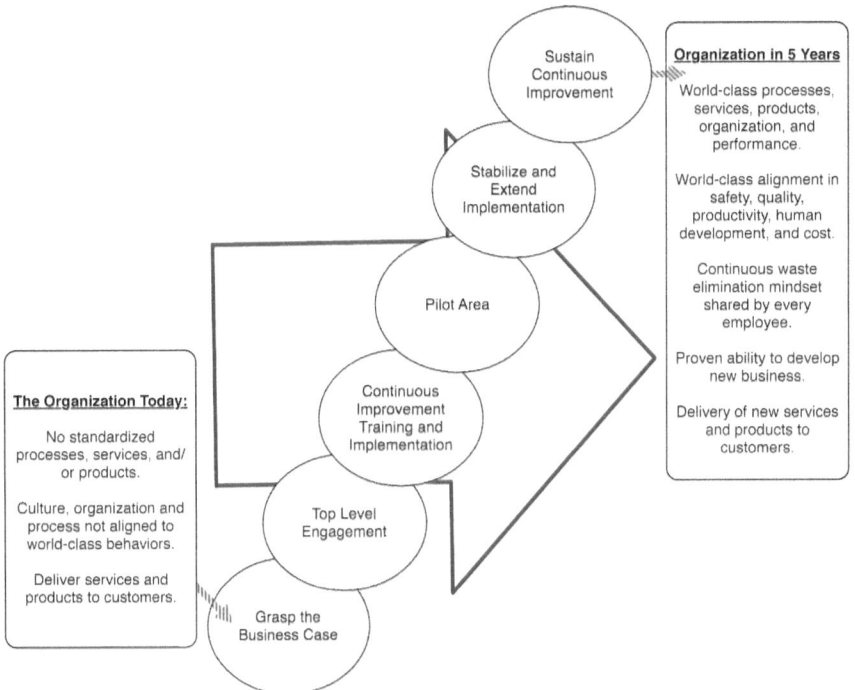

**Figure 1.2**

Grasping the business case means understanding what the business is dealing with and understanding the culture of both the industry and the organization. This starts with grasping the most prominent behaviors within the organization—both the good and the bad—in order to determine what negative behaviors to address and what positive behaviors to leverage. Understanding the organization from a value/non-value added standpoint is critical to grasping its level of efficiency.

In order for a sensei to agree to change an organization, due diligence is needed, just as it is when a prospective buyer is looking at acquiring a new company. Most organizations have one-third value added at best. Depending on the type of organization, the sensei may look to see if and in what capacity people are creating value.

### Engaging the Top-Level Team

Generally, leadership implements the tools in the Transformation Curve, first by adapting them and then by using them in the pilot hall to reinforce behaviors at the front line. Overlapping the curve, the top-level team must understand the Journey to World Class and the Transformation Curve. The goal is to learn how to lead from the top and the bottom, first in the pilot area using and coaching the tools, all while applying the organization's strategy using the Transformation Curve and daily behaviors throughout the system to get results and develop people.

### Continuous Improvement Training and Implementation

Initial training and implementation includes grasping the Continuous Improvement Program (CIP) and the appropriate Level A tools needed to communicate and train the entire organization per the plan. Implementation includes selecting and developing a continuous improvement team and establishing how it will support the executive team, pilot hall, and the remainder of the organization. Overall, the CIP includes individual suggestions, team suggestions, kaizen events, and quality control circles. Each level of the CIP is introduced within a tool of the Transformation Curve.

### The Pilot Area

A pilot is essentially a model area or team that adapts the toolbox and exhibits specific behaviors. The organization can't shift from the current state to one unified standard all at once, as it would be nearly impossible to pay for all the training and change daily behaviors at every level simultaneously. Without pilot areas to set the example and demonstrate that the tools are working and the culture is thriving, the organization will fail.

The pilot area might be a pilot team, a site team, or even a division. In some cases, the entire organization may be the pilot. The bigger the organization, the bigger the pilot needs to be to help spread the word and train the mass of the organization. Depending on the reach, the pilot division or site may also have a pilot frontline area.

### Stabilizing and Extending Implementation

As different areas of the organization see the success of the pilot and executive leaders begin to have pilot areas of their own, the learning and culture spread.

Additionally, when the initial pilot hall embraces a new tool, it first masters it before coaching someone else. The new tools are all linked so that they connect back to previous tools and lay the groundwork for other more advanced tools, all with the purpose of seeing and solving more problems.

Eventually, every department will have a pilot, whether it's the entire department or a process within the department. Pilots are necessary in all areas of the organization, both in departments that directly impact the process and in departments that support the main processes. Engineering, quality, and finance too must grasp how the tools and behaviors apply to their work so they also can support organizational transformation.

As the tools of Levels A through C help stabilize change, the system spreads throughout the organization, with tools beyond Phase One linked with strategies for extending implementation. Only organizational strategy is discussed in this book because executives must grasp and implement Level A and the management cycle at the top level prior to implementing the curve deeply with extending strategies.

## SUSTAINING CONTINUOUS IMPROVEMENT

Many organizations are able to rise to world-class status, but sustaining this status is much more difficult. When starting the Journey to World Class, leaders must grasp that in the daily living phase, nearly all problems will be solved using the basic 5 Whys (embedded in problem solving one) and simple suggestions (introduced in Phase One). Additionally, problems are solved "right now," not after a team is put together or after someone finds time to look into a problem. Having the problem-solving mentality ingrained in the culture and leaders who reinforce the culture on a daily basis are key to sustaining the gains. Even though more and more advanced tools are introduced to solve more complex problems, the system must always be sustained.

This book also briefly touches upon using maturity audits to sustain world class. This is a complex, three-phase process of auditing the operational and human systems that aims at keeping the organization multifunctional and processes ever improving. Tools in Phase Three help even further to sustain world class, but world class can never be sustained without Phase One in place.

Once the tools of the Transformation Curve are linked to daily behaviors, organizations have world-class processes, services, products, and performance. Man, machine, material, and method are all aligned to eliminate waste. Everyone has a continuous waste elimination mindset, and it becomes part of daily living to engage in improving how work is done. When an organization reaches this level, people trust the sensei and leader. There is mutual trust and respect, and looking for waste elimination becomes constant.

## The Focus of This Book

As mentioned, *The Transformation Curve to World-Class* focuses on Phase One, Levels A and B, and Phase Two, Level C only. The reasons are three-fold. First, the executive team must have an understanding of Levels A through C to begin creating an organization strategy and communicating a long-term plan. Second, the pilot hall must implement A through C quickly to become a model area. Third, everyone in the organization will be exposed to and use Level A and parts of Level B.

The management cycle, infrastructure strategy, and the remainder of the curve are not discussed in significant detail in this book because of the basic understanding of the system that is necessary prior to implementation. Without Level A in place at the executive level and a pilot area that is pursuing Levels B and C, the management cycle should not be applied.

*The Transformation Curve to World-Class* takes Levels A through C and overlaps their respective tools with engaging the top-level team, continuous improvement training and implementation, and the pilot area; it also briefly touches upon strategies to stabilize, extend, and sustain continuous improvement, as the following chapters convey.

# Chapter 2

# Phase One Tools for Top-Level Engagement

Prior to introducing the Phase One tools for top-level engagement, executives themselves must be primed for success. First and foremost, this means engaging a sensei.

## Engaging Executives with a Sensei

A sensei, a person experienced with the journey who has not only been down the road to world class but who has started with a systematic plan, should be chosen to help guide the organization directly or indirectly. The role of the sensei involves making sure that the organization's leader (chairman, president, CEO, etc.) understands all the system's cultural/behavioral elements as well as the operational tools. The sensei must be a true expert on the systematic approach—the Transformation Curve—and the leader must fully commit to the tools and the sensei throughout each phase of the process.

The sensei must be able to coach the long-term strategic plan at all levels of the organization. S/he has to bridge the gap between lower-level staff and top management by supporting the team of internal coaches—the continuous improvement team—and having necessary conversations with the executive leader about the behaviors needed to drive cultural change.

A sensei may not know the specifics of the organization—customers, suppliers, business model, metrics—but s/he should know how to ask the right questions, using the system, to get the answers necessary for organizational transformation.

Likewise, the sensei may not know key process requirements and how to design a process that's most appropriate for the organization and customers, but s/he should know how to facilitate and ask leading questions that eliminate waste and respect people. Setting waste-reduction targets, focusing on the process of improvement, and concentrating on the positives are necessary traits to help the executive team make master plans for improvement. These elements affect not only the plan for systematic implementation but also the master plans necessary to achieve the executive team's objectives as related to organization-wide goals.

## How to Choose a Sensei

Searching for and choosing a sensei can be challenging, but selecting the right person is essential. A sensei is not just someone from Toyota, any world-class organization, or an organization that has become Lean. Many organizations become Lean by linking all the tools together over time without using a systematic approach. While these organizations may achieve world-class results, this doesn't mean their leaders have long-term systematic plans that are repeatable. They may exit a Lean organization knowing Lean, how to lead a specific tool, or how to manage as an executive in that specific organization's system, but that doesn't mean they know how to change an organization's culture for the long-term or how to coach the tools in a systematic fashion linked to behaviors. This isn't due to incompetence but rather a lack of experience with a long-term approach to changing organizations.

Many successful Lean leaders, leaders from Toyota, or other Lean consultants experience the pitfalls of coming into a new organization with a different culture and failing to enact the expected change or seeing the change occur extremely slowly. Typically, these "senseis" blame the people—incompetent leaders and/or an undedicated staff—while leadership blames the plan's instigator. However, this type of "sensei" isn't really a sensei because s/he didn't have a long-term plan that could be successfully carried out and didn't know which tools to use or when, how, or where to use them.

It's also possible that the one leading transformation didn't know how to communicate positive changes in order to spread even more positive change. Organizations must be careful when choosing a sensei, as these individuals must not only have experience with traditional Lean tools and process improvement activities but must also be able to communicate and apply a long-term, repeatable approach.

Many people try to copy effective transformation leaders understand production system by copying the tools. Unfortunately, the tools alone will not yield transformation. The long-term approach will also not yield transformation when used in isolation. The key resides in coaching and creating the organization's culture.

Toyota understands that an organization can't simply copy the approach and be successful. Even many who claim to be "senseis" don't know how to link all the tools—the master planning cycles, the balanced scorecard, the suggestion system, etc.—with the organization's strategy and then use the tools to drive cultural change.

Even at Toyota, few people can effectively integrate all the steps. This is because, for most employees, this skill is unnecessary and therefore unlearned. At Toyota and many Lean organizations, the strategy and culture are already linked—these organizations are in the daily living phase, and their leaders only need to ensure they grasp the overlapping portion of teamwork so they can support the teams above, below, and side to side. Meaning, the systems and processes of producing world-class products and services have already been transformed.

This is why a true sensei must have already made the journey, a journey with an end-goal of becoming world class as defined by the long-term scorecard, initially five to six years out. The sensei must have a long-term strategic plan that has been both applied and improved upon. If a sensei gives an organization the same plan s/he gave a different organization five years ago, it means s/he hasn't learned and adapted to make improvements. S/he must have already been down the pathway using the long-term strategic plan, not theoretically, not as a team member or an executive, but as a coach or sensei. If s/he doesn't have a proven track record for affecting organizational change—not just changing processes—executives must find a sensei who does.

Eventually, the executive leader, executive team, and CIP must mimic the coaching and behavior taught and demonstrated by the sensei. One of the sensei's goals is to create "mini-senseis" within the organization, typically starting with the continuous improvement team and pilot hall. If the sensei does not build a team of others who can coach the system, s/he has failed. This is why a sensei must know how to manage all the overlaps and coach the right tools at the right time in order to help other leaders also manage the overlaps.

The sensei in turn needs an executive leader to enact the system or at least support it. The leader may not need to do/implement all the tools completely, but this individual must deeply understand how each tool is linked, know how to coach the tools, and especially know how to lead with them and through them.

A great executive leader is a role model for balancing the human and operational aspects of the organization through daily behavior. If an executive doesn't demonstrate the behaviors necessary to build mutual trust and respect and doesn't understand the tools used, it will be difficult for the organization to make it very far on the Transformation Curve and thus to be successful.

## BALANCING THE 3PS AND THE 3GS

First and foremost, executive leaders must manage the 3Ps—people, passion, and patience—and the 3Gs—go see, get the facts, and grasp the situation—so that all the leaders in the organization exhibit behaviors that support and further the human/operational balance, as seen in Figure 2.1 below.

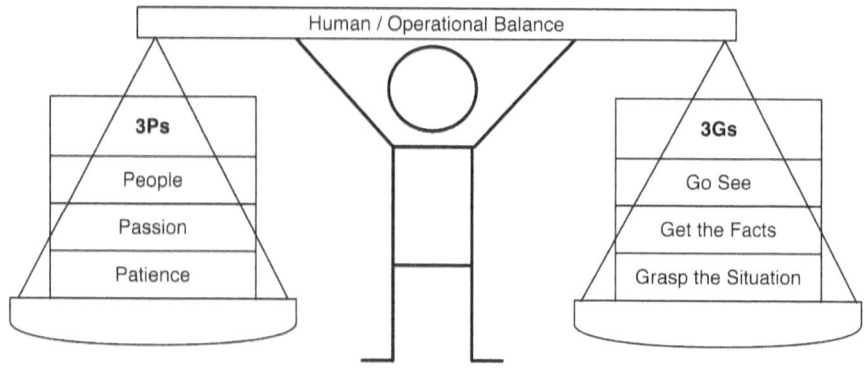

Figure 2.1

All leaders have talents and abilities that helped them reach their current positions. However, in world-class organizations with world-class cultures, everything is based on mutual trust and respect, not necessarily on the skill or behavior set that got the executive leader to where s/he is. If leaders are unable to gain the mutual trust and respect of the organization's employees, how will they gain the organization's hearts and minds to engage in improvement moving forward?

The 3Gs are typically the more memorable of the 3P/3G balance and make up the operational side of the scale. They help leaders focus on fact management, solve operational problems, and observe the actual work being done to find waste/value.

The 3Ps deal with the human side of the scale and are often minimized or diminished, causing the organization to be unbalanced. Leaders, especially executive leaders, must have a passion for improvement, must grasp that people are the true assets of the organization, and most importantly must have patience for the system and not expect cultural change to occur overnight either individually or organizationally. Executive leaders must always balance the 3Ps and 3Gs.

## Changing from Command and Control

From a cultural standpoint, most executive teams are in a "command and control" position. They understand the organization from the top down, but they don't know how to support improvement and lead transformation by leading from the middle. Their key performance indicators (KPIs) are based on financial outcomes. They are always looking for the red, which means they're always looking for problems rather than leveraging the company's success to solve more problems. They are in a very reactive mode with metrics, and when they see something that doesn't achieve a target, they immediately attack. They never address and use what has already been accomplished—the positive. The problem is, if executives are always in a negative mode, they will fail to build mutual trust and respect throughout the organization.

The most important behavior needed to facilitate organizational change is establishing mutual trust and respect using the 3Ps and 3Gs. Executives do this by embracing the management cycle dimensions, roles/responsibilities, grasping the standard (what it's going to look like in five years), and the gap analysis. No sensei or executive leader should go in on day one and tell a vice president or director something to the effect of, "These are the behaviors you need to exhibit; remember these…" and offer a list of all the necessary behaviors.

This simply won't work. At some point, all leaders have behaviors that need to end and some that need to be harnessed toward the right, positive format. The sensei's responsibility is to help leaders manage the 3Ps and 3Gs and to ensure that these leaders themselves are reinforcing positive behaviors and building mutual trust and respect. Unfortunately, most organizations never become world class because they can only point out negative behaviors and don't focus on the positive.

It may sound counterintuitive, but the leader's and sensei's role is to focus on positive behaviors in order to ultimately cast out negative ones. They do this by asking "why" questions. They go and see. They have some type of system for informal Plan-Do-Check-Act (PDCA). They are good at focusing on one specific problem. They facilitate meetings effectively. They are sticklers about time. They want others to be successful. They help their direct reports.

The right behavior from leadership builds the right momentum among top-level leaders as well as the general population of the organization. This means the sensei must hone in on the right behaviors and teach the executive leader to do the same. Executives should celebrate problem solving, celebrate creating a plan, celebrate the first monthly meeting cycle, and celebrate hitting targets. They should not focus on the red and ask what's being done about it but instead focus on the green and ask "How?" to replicate more success. They should learn from the positive and spread it. Recognizing the right behaviors at the top helps executives focus on the right behaviors with their direct reports. In short, instead of just striving for results, leaders must focus on changing behaviors by recognizing and acknowledging positive behaviors.

## Reinforcing Good Behavior at Toyota

When Rodger's sensei at Toyota was teaching him to see, he took Rodger out to the floor and said, "What do you see?"

Rodger stated the obvious and said, "I see a car going by."

His sensei replied, "Okay, cars go by everywhere; what do you see?"

Rodger saw that this car had defects and pointed that out. He pointed out the negative, i.e., the problems.

His sensei asked him again, "What do you see?"

It took Rodger a long time to realize that what he saw were positive cultural behaviors rather than defects and problems.

He saw a team leader walk up and help a team member. He saw a team member ask a team leader to take a look at something that needed checking. He saw a supervisor on the line confirming that the team leader was following the process according to his standard work.

After this experience, Rodger began seeing and looking for behaviors—positive behaviors—not simply results, and not simply problems to solve.

Learning to see is not about going up to a balanced scorecard and saying, "Why didn't you make this target? Why didn't you do 15 problem-solving sheets last month? Why didn't you have 34 suggestions implemented last month?"

Instead, learning to see is about seeing positive behaviors. If leaders can't see positive behaviors and see the improvement portion—the improvements that have already taken place—it's very difficult to coach people to close the gap between the current condition and the future desired state effectively.

Recognizing the good helps identify the next step—"What do I need to do to help improve?"—in terms of the value added process and in terms of the leadership process. It takes a real leader to find a positive. Being able to see is important, and it's just as important to know how to react to what is seen, focusing on what's already improved and the positive activity to help close the gap, not just seeing the negative portion and reacting to that.

## Leaders Must Reinforce Good Behavior

Leaders must focus on the bottom of the organization, recognizing positive improvements and asking questions to gain further improvements, gaining momentum, to shift the culture. In many cases, the bottom of the organization swings the top. The continuous improvement team helps leaders focus on the positive, reinforcing right behaviors, from the monthly performance review meeting recognizing the positive to going and seeing implemented suggestions and even recognizing employees for perfect attendance.

One chairman who used this system started each company visit by attending the top monthly meeting with his teams. This connected him with the people, their problems, and their improvements. Tellingly, the employees were always impressed when the chairman left, not because he'd come but because of how he spoke with and coached them. The chairman was managing the 3Ps and the 3Gs to build mutual trust and respect.

The cultural impact was always so impressive that, the next day, suggestions came pouring in. This is one of the many positive products produced by mutual trust and respect and is the essence of the Toyota Production System.

As with many leaders, connecting with his employees didn't come naturally for this particular leader. Rodger, as his sensei, always helped coach him, improving the leadership process and the chairman's management cycle. Such behaviors must at least be acknowledged before the sensei begins engaging the executive team in Phase One of the Transformation Curve.

## Phase One Tools for Executive Teams

The Phase One, Level A tools are shown in Figure 2.2 . They include: balanced scorecard, annual planning, improvement system, safety system, workplace organization, and problem solving one—must be learned and implemented at the executive level first. In Level A, the tools are essentially the same for the executive team as they are in the pilot hall and any other place in the organization that starts the Transformation Curve.

When an organization's leadership team starts the Transformation Curve, it starts with culture and focuses on safety and quality. It's critical that this team understands how and where to focus and the goal to reach in five or six years in terms of world-class processes, products, services, and results. Inevitably, the highest-level results are selected, checked, and visualized using balanced scorecards.

## The Balanced Scorecard

Most organizations have some sort of performance card. It may have some "balanced" information, but organizations typically use the key performance indicators linked to finance. The problem is, many executives are like bulls—they go straight for the red and focus on the negative. When they do this, it's very difficult for anyone else on the executive team or the rest of the organization to see the positive. Therefore, priorities must be balanced focusing on safety and quality first, not just financial targets.

Leadership teams must begin with world-class priorities in this order—safety, quality, productivity, human development, cost, and the systematic approach. If executives don't want to focus this way, it's very difficult to help them, because focusing on cost before safety and quality violates mutual trust and respect.

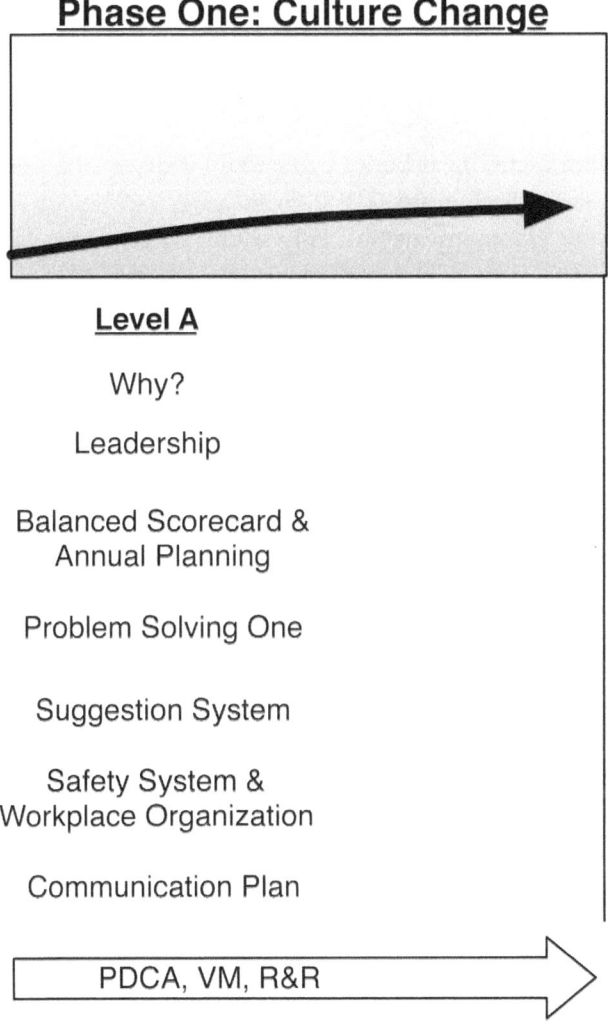

Figure 2.2

When the sensei coaches the executive team to establish a balanced scorecard, s/he needs to focus on where the organization wants to be in five or six years based on these world-class priorities. The leader must have patience and passion for transformation, while the five- or six-year scorecard links world-class characteristics with daily behaviors.

The balanced scorecard reflects a specific order for specific reasons. Safety is always the number one priority from both a results and behavioral standpoint. Quality comes before production because the rule of thumb is "Do not accept, create, or pass along poor quality."

Production comes next because generally it drives the business and the rest of the balanced scorecard.

Human development may initially address attendance or participation in the suggestion system, but in the long run, the aim of the organizational strategy will be to create a multifunctional workforce. On the Journey to World Class, human development will be used to track flexibility, cross training, and team leader qualifications all related to the organizational and team strategies. At that point, a leader would never let the process suffer in terms of quality or productivity in order to cross train team members. Thus, when organizations want to adapt the order or the words on the balanced scorecard, they must first grasp the long-term plan and understand the unintended consequences that will happen down the road as other strategies of the Transformation Curve are introduced.

The priorities—safety, quality, productivity, human development, cost, and the systematic approach—begin to create a value system that translates into behaviors. When the leadership team identifies a safety problem and a productivity problem, if all things are essentially equal, the team is charged with solving the safety problem first. If quality problems are identified that impact the customer and the line needs to stop to solve the quality problem, so be it. If production is behind schedule and overtime is necessary to avoid impacting delivery to the customer, cost may suffer to support productivity. This doesn't mean that safety trumps quality or that productivity trumps cost—it means there is a balance. However, the priorities in that order can be turned into daily behaviors.

## SIX-YEAR BALANCED SCORECARD

The sensei must help executive leaders reach their objectives and make PDCA cycles based on those objectives part of daily living. The sensei coaches the executive team to plan five years ahead, because while all companies would like to be world class, it's very difficult to move from the current state to world class overnight. Interim—annual—targets are thus established as waypoints. Everyone wants to have zero accidents, but is that realistic? Putting "zero" as a goal on the balanced scorecard for the first year means everybody will fail, including the system. Therefore, the long-range or "true north" target is zero, but realistically, this goal is attained over a series of years.

For example, from a quality standpoint, if there are currently 10 defects per product, while 3 defects qualify as world class, yearly targets may be set at 9, 8, 6, 5, 4, and 3 over six years, as shown in Figure 2.3 below.

| Priority | Objective | R | S | Metrics | Baseline | 2015 | 2016 | 2017 | 2018 | 2019 | 2020 | World-Class |
|---|---|---|---|---|---|---|---|---|---|---|---|---|
| Safety | To be world-class in safety. | RBL | SL | OSHA Rate | 2 | 2 | 1.5 | 1 | 0.5 | 0.25 | 0.1 | 0.1 |

**Figure 2.3**

If executives set unattainable targets, they will fail and lose trust in the system. The system, through the six-year balanced scorecard, helps executives identify what is world class for safety, quality, and so on and gives them the opportunity to be successful while reinforcing the positive.

At Toyota, true north is always the same. It's employee satisfaction, customer satisfaction, community satisfaction, and the success of the enterprise. Everyone knows this and no one loses sight of it. It's ingrained into Toyota's culture.

However, an organization can't copy Toyota's true north without establishing organizational objectives and aligning the balanced scorecard to strategy. The point of true north is the same—being world class. The elements of how and when to get there vary.

Toyota seeks true north in all things. It isn't going to build a car that doesn't point true north. It isn't going to build a truck that's not true north. It knows that true north is the goal. The goal is not to beat GM or Ford, because if the employees, suppliers, and customers are engaged, learning, becoming multifunctional, and supported, everybody wins. On the Journey to World Class, the sensei recognizes that the organization must change gradually rather than immediately.

Some organizations try to copy Toyota's definition of true north without adapting it to their own organizations. As mentioned, merely copying Toyota is never the best strategy. Trying to start out with true north targets may paint a picture that is unattainable and not linked to concrete plans. Rodger knew he didn't want to just imitate Toyota, so he adapted true north to world class and used the six-year balanced scorecard.

Using the Transformation Curve and establishing long-term metrics linked to world class is key—these metrics are achievable when linked with the long-term plan. Some organizations are good at recasting metrics year after year, but this can make the end goal unclear. If a measure is changing from one year to the next, it can lose its value. The six-year balanced scorecard helps focus executive teams and links world-class outcomes to daily behaviors.

*Balanced Scoreboard*

Once the long-term, world-class targets are established along with the first year's target, the sensei coaches the executive team to visualize the target over the year, at least monthly, and to establish PDCA cycles around the balanced scorecard.

The tool used to visualize these targets, top problems, and proactive indicators is a balanced scoreboard. This proactive improvement tool is shown in Figure 2.4 below and is the framework for teams to showcase their positive improvements linked to the annual plan and activities linked to achieving the balanced scorecard targets.

|  | SAFETY | QUALITY | PRODUCTIVITY | HUMAN DEVELOPMENT | COST | OPERATIONAL EXCELLENCE |
|---|---|---|---|---|---|---|
| Metrics |  |  |  |  |  |  |
| Top 3 Problems |  |  |  |  |  |  |
| Problem Solving Sheets |  |  |  |  |  |  |
| Support |  |  |  |  |  |  |

**Figure 2.4**

The top row links with the six-year scorecard and the bottom row indicates either support or proactive measures to drive the top row. This scorecard is a centerpiece that links daily problem solving with world-class outcomes and is one tool to help increase visual management.

The top row of the scoreboard is helpful in visualizing the one-year targets of the six-year balanced scorecard. Generally, this row is limited to 18 key performance indicators—a maximum of 3 in each priority—so that the scorecard remains balanced and focused.

Metrics should be tracked at least monthly, as the monthly meeting is one of the first checkpoints established. The second and third rows on the balanced scoreboard are for top problems and are a way to visually display the priority problems that have been solved. A good sensei will coach teams to display top problems in a sequence—first identifying problems, then offering more specific problem statements, and eventually defining complex problems.

In the beginning, keeping it simple is key so that problems can be successfully solved and the balanced scoreboard is used as an improvement tool to showcase the positive changes the team has mastered.

If the leader understands the system and business deeply, the executive team may not have a proactive fourth row immediately. The sensei may let executives put things in the fourth row they feel comfortable with tracking to highlight the positive changes generated from top problems. Managing the fourth row of the balanced scorecard proactively, all the while focusing on process, is a way to move towards the outcomes, but executives must be empowered to identify the fourth row key performance indicators on their own. Once they do this, it's easier to manage the fourth row and thus the outcomes linked to the six-year balanced scorecard and daily behaviors.

The sensei and leaders must know what needs to be done in order to achieve the target, because if leaders set unattainable targets or do not know how to support their teams by using their toolbox, the organization and people are set up for failure. Leaders won't be able to see success—they will just see failure and become uninspired. If they are uninspired, they will be unengaged and unable to drive the cultural change necessary to become world class. This is why, especially in the first years, the balanced scorecard must be set up to achieve success. Once people smell success, they know what it takes, they feel good, and they know they can do it again. The key is to set targets that can be achieved in the first year. Then, once people are enabled and engaged, the targets can be more of a challenge that teams will rise to meet.

*Daily Morning Meetings*

The daily meeting is typically a short stand-up meeting in front of the scoreboard that links the six-year balanced scorecard with daily activities and problem solving. During the first daily meetings, the sensei must focus on observing and grasping behaviors, both positive and negative, to establish a coaching plan. Artifacts are present such as the scoreboard, key performance indicators, and problem sheets, but a good sensei is really observing behaviors. Are people on their cell phones? Are they late for the meeting? How is their posture? Are they asking positive or negative questions?

The sensei must get the executive team to focus on the positives and look for behaviors that reinforce them. When these behaviors are in place, the team can begin to solve problems, which is the number one key to leadership.

The purpose of the meeting is to review daily key performance indicators linked to the six-year scorecard both reactively and proactively. In the beginning, many of the key performance indicators may be reactive, reporting on what happened the day before and using problem solving to respond. Being reactive should only occur until the executive team begins to understand which proactive measures must be put in place. These proactive activities are then visualized on the fourth row of the scoreboard.

For example, workforce safety is a balanced scorecard metric, so a question at the first daily meetings might be, "Did any safety incidents occur yesterday? If so, what were they?"

Answers to these questions must be linked to the problem-solving and suggestion systems, ensuring that daily meetings are not merely a report on the negative. Solving problems and implementing improvements helps teams focus on action and the positive. Eventually, when proactive checks are put in place, instead of the executive team's question about workforce safety events, an executive might ask for a report on the status and findings of the last safety audit conducted on the floor. Go and sees will begin to occur immediately after the daily meeting.

Eventually, the sensei may suggest an afternoon meeting so the team can be even more proactive on a daily basis, identifying what measures must be in place for the next shift and the next day. I.e., are all the people needed for tomorrow in place? Are machines running as planned to support the process? Are all the supplies/equipment in place in order to support the process for the next shift and the next day?

Thus begins a proactive approach to problem solving, yet most teams need to start with reactive problem solving to learn the approach and problem-solving thinking.

## Problem Solving One

In the beginning, leaders often treat problems as individual failures. If there's a problem, they think it's because someone didn't do something. In other words, it's someone's fault. But when the focus is on building mutual trust and respect, people are not the problem, nor do people make defects. It's the process that produces problems.

Getting the leadership team to see that problems are opportunities for improvement and not people related is key. The sensei should never let an executive or anyone else define a problem as a person. It's always a process.

In the early days, the leader and sensei need to make sure that everyone is clear on this: the organization has good people and good products/services—it's the process that needs changing. People will change too, of course, but the focus is on changing the process.

If the team sees a problem, it should improve the process using a systematic approach. First comes simple problem solving (problem solving one), then more advanced problem solving (problem solving two). If a person makes a mistake, it's because the process isn't clear. Typically, the standard is incorrect or missing or there's a problem with the check portion, which makes it a management/leadership process.

Changing the concept from "problems are bad" to "problems are blessings" helps leaders focus on process control or process identification of the problem and keeps their focus away from people. Along those lines, leaders need to make it clear that people will not be crucified for articulating a problem and/or starting a problem-solving sheet, which is further discussed below.

### *Problems Are Blessings*

To reiterate, problems must be celebrated in order for people to see them as blessings. It's not enough for leaders to simply state that problems are opportunities for improvements. Many current and former Toyota leaders share stories of the first problem they experienced and their first "andon pull" on the assembly line as well as the ceremonial way other team members and their team leader celebrated the identification of the problem.

Though an andon system will not yet be in place because the organization is just learning about problem solving, senseis must celebrate the exposure of problems in a similar fashion during the first daily meetings. Leaders must then perpetuate the positive attitude surrounding problems as they begin to use the system in the pilot and around the organization.

In the beginning, it's not just about solving problems but also about teaching leaders how to do simple problem solving and to follow through with countermeasures. Focusing on smaller problems is key to teaching problem solving. Instead of trying to solve the problem of "On time deliveries are at 60%," for example, the team should initially focus on a simpler problem such as, "A defect yesterday in the assembly department led to a shipment being late." Focusing on small yet impactful problems helps teams get through the entire problem-solving process—a PDCA cycle. This too will help with the overall problem of a missed target such as a 60% defect rate.

The human and operational side of problem solving must be in balance—if problems are not actually being solved but only identified, mutual trust and respect will not be promoted. Many problems, especially in the beginning, are the result of insufficient, incorrect, or missing standards. Therefore, the root cause of most problems deals with standards, and countermeasures typically address the gap of standardization, no matter how small.

The goal is not to standardize work but rather to get people in a problem-solving mindset and to teach them problem-solving methodology. Doing this efficiently and effectively requires an organizational standard for simple problem solving.

### The Problem-Solving Sheet

The organization must have a tool to help visualize and solve problems using a systematic process. This tool might be a note pad, flip chart, problem-solving sheet, or something else. The actual tool is not as important as the coaching and learning cycles that accompany it.

Having a standard tool to identify specific problems and a mechanism for follow-up is critical. It may sound simple, but identifying the problem plus who is responsible for solving it, who is responsible for supporting this individual, and the timeframe for solving it is key.

The problem-solving sheet, seen in Figure 2.5 below, creates a standard that can be coached and linked to the rest of the system.

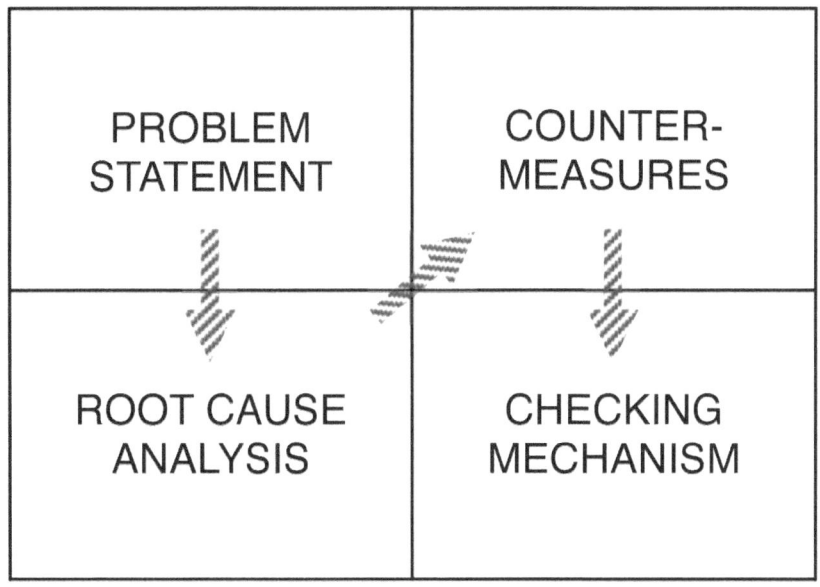

**Figure 2.5**

Problem solving starts with problem identification and more specifically the point at which the problem is recognized, the point where the problem initially occurs, and a specific statement of facts to describe the problem. Root cause analysis—asking why five times—is used to help identify the causal link about the underlying reason for the problem. This root cause informs the development of a countermeasure, a long-term activity to keep the problem from happening again. The checking mechanism, visualized in the bottom right side of the problem-solving sheet, is a visualization of the recurrence of the actual problem or the root cause of the problem.

Reporting out and solving problems must be done daily. An everyday problem-solving activity must be linked to the daily meeting until it becomes part of daily living. Ultimately, there needs to be a visual method to monitor the status of problems from where the work is done. That visual method may be a tool to help visualize the status of problems or the plan for how quickly countermeasures will be implemented. Regardless of the tool, it must help the leader see and enforce a PDCA cycle of solving problems.

Many organizations begin with A3s instead of simple problem-solving sheets. They are essentially copying Toyota, but at Toyota, where the 5 Whys are done in teams with leaders, simple problem solving is part of daily living. That's the way it is, and the people who work, are hired, and promoted within Toyota understand this process. But at most organizations that are not world class, the 5 Whys are not inherent or ingrained in the culture. The people don't deeply understand how to do a root cause analysis on paper, let alone in their heads. That's why a tool like the problem-solving sheet can help teach leaders simple PDCA and the basics of problem solving and begin to build a culture of problem solvers on a daily basis.

## *PDCA AND PROBLEM SOLVING ONE*

Teaching PDCA using problem statements, root cause analysis, developing countermeasures, and checking those countermeasures through solving problems is key in problem solving one. For example, if the leader articulates that a root cause and countermeasure will be identified and implemented by Wednesday, then on Wednesday that problem must be solved. Ultimately, it's the responsibility of the leader to coach, check, and celebrate. The leader can't simply demand that a problem sheet be completed and check that it's done; s/he must also support the process.

Executive leaders need to make sure there's a plan so that their team members can be successful in solving the problem, all while coaching their team members as needed. Asking the right questions using PDCA and selecting the right problems linked to the balanced scorecard, in particular the fourth row, helps people realize that if they don't solve the problem, they will not achieve their fourth row key performance indicators and therefore will not achieve the outcomes. Leaders also link the "go and sees" with the problem-solving sheets, using them as a guide to ask questions and engage team members in solving the problems.

Once the organizations and specific leaders get comfortable using the 5 Whys, they can start with more advanced tools to build upon problem solving one. Much more advanced problem-solving tools can build off of problem solving one including a Fishbone or a Pareto Chart, then maybe an advanced Six Sigma project. But leaders have to start with the basics first, building the skills to help the organization solve problems on a daily basis.

*Top Problems on the Scoreboard*

Once the executive team embraces problem solving, especially problem identification, the sensei can teach them how to wrap PDCA cycles around problem solving and how to use monthly check cycles to link problem prioritization with the annual plan.

To begin, using the Transformation Curve, the sensei typically tells a leadership team to start a problem-solving sheet for every single existing problem. Introducing a culture of problem solving is the purpose, not necessarily identifying and solving every single problem.

At one organization, Rodger received 7,000 problem-solving sheets after communicating the standard—a problem sheet for every problem. Essentially, the problem-solving sheets were not important as a problem-solving tool but as a learning tool. With the problems visualized and documented, Rodger could coach and teach leaders how to prioritize and begin solving the right problems using PDCA. This is one way to begin the monthly meeting cycle, a cycle that begins to link daily activity with six-year targets.

## Monthly Meetings to Link the Scoreboard and Problem Solving One

Typically, leaders shouldn't start the monthly meetings until the teams (leadership or pilot) are comfortable with the daily meeting. The sensei must establish clear and simple checks of the Level A system components looking for things like balanced scorecards, attendance at meetings, and visual charts. Once these things work well and executives feel comfortable, the sensei can lead the team into a monthly scorecard review to check where they are inconsistent with annual objectives and daily problem solving.

The target is not to have a monthly meeting at all levels of the organization but at least to have the monthly meeting with leadership and the pilot hall(s). Once the leadership level monthly meeting is working, the purpose becomes to check whether or not the right key performance indicators are in place on the fourth row to manage problems proactively so that the balanced scorecard target is achieved next month.

By moving to monthly meetings, the top-level team moves first, then the pilot, and then other parts of the organization begin to see and mimic that. Once they see that it's about being proactive, the monthly meeting won't have to occur everywhere formally.

During this phase, the role of the Continuous Improvement Program team (the CIP is discussed in depth in Chapter Three) is to listen throughout the organization and to guide executives and the sensei (depending on the relationship) on top problem selection.

If executives choose very complex problems that will take a year to solve, the sensei and CIP team can help to focus on a particular problem statement. If the executive team focuses only on the problems that aren't solved, the sensei or CIP team leader can help them focus on the problems they have solved that they should be monitoring and helping to spread. If the executive team seems to be choosing problems that may not necessarily be the best problems to focus on, the sensei can guide them by asking questions and pointing out other potential top problems. The key is for the continuous improvement team leader to be patient as the team moves from reactive to proactive and from negative to positive.

## Annual Planning

Many leaders and organizations complete balanced scorecards, strategic planning, and budgets during one month a year, thinking, "We need a budget for this year and a strategic plan."

But if the organization and leader have a balanced scorecard and established five-year targets, they can look at and adapt the key performance indicators for five years to the balanced scorecard, taking into consideration the strategic plan and business. Then the annual planning cycles and PDCA cycle are simply checking along the lines of, "Have I achieved my goal to date? If not, what must I do to catch up? Are we on track to meet next year's targets?"

That's why leaders shouldn't wait until the end of the year to check and do the annual or strategic plan. Using the Toyota Production System, when it's time to do annual planning, executives should already recognize the problems from the year and be proactive in order to address them. Then they can look at what's different for next year—what needs to be adjusted to account for the changes. The check and adjust cycles must be integrated into the monthly meeting, quarterly checks, and eventually daily living.

In a world-class business, annual planning is nothing but an andon—a proactive mechanism to signal for help. If the PDCA cycle is working, andon is working within the annual plan and leaders won't find themselves significantly short with three months left in the year and no time to make up for it. They will know when there is a discrepancy between the annual and six-year goals and be able to enact countermeasures.

In world-class organizations, the true goal of annual planning is to have a plan by the hour so that if the team misses the target this hour, they can achieve it next hour. There's only so much that can be picked up hourly, so the goal is never to let the deficit run over to the next shift. By extension, if the deficit doesn't run over to the next shift, it won't run over to the next week, next month, next quarter, etc. That means in world-class organizations, leaders, teams, and the organization are doing PDCA on the annual plan by the hour.

*Annual Master Plan*

When starting the annual planning cycle, introducing a simple tool like a master plan helps leaders visualize the plan and gives the sensei an artifact to coach. The master plan is an 11 x 17 sheet of paper that lists the master schedule, the activities needed to achieve the objective, who is responsible for and supporting each activity, and the general timing.

The controller of the master plan visualizes the planned timing of each activity and shades in the timeline and status report for each activity. The purpose of these plans is to create objectives on the six-year balanced scorecard and to link those objectives with plans to achieve them by visualizing the plan and its checks. Too many organizations create objectives and goals but lack the discipline to create a detailed plan and check that plan on a frequent basis—not only the results but also the activities needed to achieve the results.

Initially, leaders may believe they don't need to know when specifics of the plan will occur. They will be hesitant to commit to a number of weeks or a general timeframe. To combat this, begin with a visual plan. Check the plan. Eventually, when the balanced scoreboard is a check of the results and proactive KPIs that link to the results, the master plan will be used as a control tool.

### *Master Planning As a Control Tool*

In terms of linking the balanced scoreboard cycle and the annual planning cycle, the scoreboard is an improvement tool and the master plan is a control tool.

If a leader or employee approaches the balanced scoreboard saying, "When are you going to do this? Why haven't you completed that?" it generally means the master planning process isn't working as it should be—as a control tool.

There must be a balance between control and reinforcing positives. The purpose of the balanced scoreboard is to point out the positives and celebrate the activities that have been completed. The sensei may observe that tasks are not being completed on time and may wonder why, but s/he will keep those questions until the master planning cycle to ensure that the appropriate countermeasures/activities are on someone's master plan.

During the initial annual planning cycle especially, leaders must focus on positives and coach planning, celebrating that people have plans and celebrating when the plans reflect more and more detail. In more mature stages of annual planning, when the other tools are linked and working, the master plan checkpoints will become much more of a control tool. Leaders can hone in on specific plans based on balanced scorecard results, one-page reports, and problem-solving sheets. The rest of the system will inform the leaders what they must do in terms of command/control to support organizational transformation.

## Executives Must Grasp Level A and Part of Level B

The rest of the Transformation Curve can be coached or implemented on a case-by-case basis, but executives must be able to master certain tools, including all of Level A and part of Level B. For example, executives who can't do a 5S and the 5 Whys will not be able to coach the workforce to find the cause of a problem. If an executive cannot understand a balanced scorecard, it's difficult to coach leading and lagging indicators as well as proactive problem solving. This is why executives must understand and use Levels A and B very well and the other levels case by case.

Specific tools in the toolbox only require specific people to be experts in using them, but every leader has to be an expert in Levels A and B. If executives can't actually help somebody create a problem statement without using command and control, they can't lead, and the organization will be stagnant.

Leaders, including quality, finance, production, etc., need to master Levels A and B.

If an organization is using the curve and has the proper sensei and a committed executive leader, the other executives are theoretically easy to change because the executive leader controls their evaluations. If the leader/sensei has control of defining the criteria of the evaluation, s/he has control of the executive team.

The evaluation check should consist of the balanced scorecard, the master plans, problem solving, and other Phase One tools. The sensei/leader defines the check and can have face-to-face conversations to control the behaviors necessary to support the curve on a daily basis.

Roles and responsibilities come from the behaviors on evaluations, the balanced scorecard becomes the objective, and the master plan links to the objective as a means to achieve it. If leaders can't or won't do such basic things as create a master plan, utilize a balanced scorecard, and embrace problem solving, they will force themselves out as the organization moves forward.

## Not Every Leader Can Oversee the System, But Can They Support It?

Executive leaders must understand strategic planning, the annual cycle, the foundations of the curve, the PDCA cycle, roles and responsibilities, and the management cycle. Leaders must understand the leadership framework and grasp the necessity of beginning to solve every problem from the middle, deciding the best leadership approach. Leaders can't always get the results they'd like, but they need to know which tools will be the most effective, where to apply them, and either how to implement them or how to coach others to implement them. These skills are the essence of learning to see and coach a systematic approach.

The system isn't made for everyone, but every leader must be able to support and/or coach it, if not do it. I.e., not everyone is able to perform structured PDCA and truly embrace the Transformation Curve, but that doesn't mean they can't survive within the system.

One leader said to Rodger, "You see a lot of opportunities," and asked to accompany him on his go-and-sees. This leader was a person whose heart embraced the system but who struggled to get his head to follow suit. He tried every day to implement the system. He was a big supporter and he believed, but he was too technically minded to succeed. Everybody knew this, and nearly everybody respected him because he knew this about himself. Some people thought he didn't fit the system because he was too humanistic, but if he'd been fired, the organization would have rejected a man who believed in and supported the system but who, due to his chemistry, couldn't fully lead it.

On the other hand, some people simply refuse to embrace the system. Typically, in such cases, the system does the firing. Once the standard is clear that leaders must use a balanced scorecard and create a master plan, it becomes clear who is and is not embracing the system. When master plan reviews reveal that executives aren't doing what's right, their peers apply so much pressure that they leave. If that doesn't happen, the tools in the system can be used to help alter their work. Master planning, balanced scorecards, 3Gs, 3Ps, and putting the management cycle dimensions on their evaluations make clear which behaviors are expected.

One person Rodger helped coach left because he actively resisted teamwork and the system to support it and couldn't/wouldn't help his peers. After his peers put pressure on him, he left, not because he wasn't part of the team but because he wouldn't use teamwork. No one told him he was bad or had to leave; on the contrary, the leaders used the system to force him to change or to leave on his own.

That's the best way for leaders to handle such situations. Beating people up doesn't work and brings negativity to everyone, while building the management cycle dimensions into performance evaluations and having face-to-face discussions about performance and behavioral expectations does.

Altogether, many of the Phase One, Level A tools—understanding why, leadership, the balanced scorecard, annual planning, and problem solving one along with the supporting tools—must be embraced and adapted by leadership before the rest of Level A can be grasped.

Other tools of Level A include the improvement system, safety system, workplace organization, and the communication plan, which must be established by the executive team to communicate the tools of Level A throughout the organization.

Before the communication plan can be implemented, as the next chapter makes clear, there must be a person or team dedicated to continuous improvement training and implementation, otherwise known as the continuous improvement team.

# Chapter 3

# Continuous Improvement Training and Implementation

Generally, everyone in the organization, at least everyone in the same facility as the pilot hall, should be exposed to the Level A tools introduced in the previous chapter as quickly as possible per the plan. Ultimately, the size of the organization and the pace of planned organizational transformation will dictate who gets what tools at what point. Leaders must be sure to stay focused on the pilot hall but to communicate these tools. Before this important communication plan can be implemented, the Continuous Improvement Program (CIP) and team need to come together.

## The Continuous Improvement Team

CIP team members must be experts, just like the sensei. Generally, these people are the internal experts, learning how each specific tool works within the system and coaching it at their level to support the program. This team has to look at the tools in the toolbox and grasp the strategic plan. Team members must understand how to link the tools, the culture, and the strategic plan to move the organization towards achieving the goals and objectives on the balanced scorecard.

It isn't simply about having someone who knows how to do Lean. Rather, it's about having someone who is business orientated, sensitive to the human/cultural side of the organization, and understands how to help move the organization forward. The leader of the Continuous Improvement Program must also embody mutual trust and respect and manage both the 3Ps and 3Gs.

## Selecting the Continuous Improvement Team

Leaders need to be very careful when selecting CIP team members; they can't just hire people who look like them. Team members must be brought into the culture who are willing to learn the tools in a new way. If team members are hired because they have a multicolored belt (Yellow Belts, Green Belts, Black Belts, etc.) or because they have studied Lean for years or are self-proclaimed "Lean experts," organizations must be even more cautious. Many of these people come with preconceived notions of how things should be and how the tools work without grasping the entire system, the cultural enablers, and the long-term plan.

Hiring leaders from other world-class organizations to this team can also be a mistake. Just because individuals thrive in world-class organizations elsewhere doesn't mean they can be successful in a new organization where they are expected to change behaviors and sequence traditional tools in order to change culture and achieve results.

In fact, many individuals from very successful organizations take positions within other organizations only to find they can't function. They know what "world class" looks and feels like, but they can't coach leadership to get there. Many of these same leaders get frustrated and exit traditional organizations in order to find different world-class organizations in which their individual performance will be better, thanks to the system that surrounds them.

Getting the right type of person on the CIP team is critical for the success of the transformation. In general, it's usually best not to hire outsiders. They may have previous knowledge of the Toyota Production System (TPS), Lean, and Six Sigma, but they won't be able to apply TPS because they don't know the organization's culture.

People on the inside already understand how the culture works daily and can help the sensei see where to focus, while the sensei can teach them. The sensei can coach the CIP leader about the tools and how to use them, but this leader must already understand the culture.

People who think they are experts who already know everything shouldn't be hired to the CIP team, either. It doesn't mean they are bad people, but the sensei and leader will spend more time changing their behavior than they can afford to spend. Hiring people who understand a toolbox (or think they do) but do not promote mutual trust and respect or being world class in behavior will never benefit the company. They will tell you why something won't work instead of trying to understand and make it work. These people cause a ruckus, don't want to learn the system, and generally make the sensei, the leader, and the system look bad.

When establishing the CIP team and bringing new team members into the organization as the system progresses, the Stars Matrix, summarized in Figure 3.1, helps ensure from a behavioral standpoint that people will mesh with the company's culture and promote mutual trust and respect.

| Traditional | World-Class |
|---|---|
| Education | Values |
| Fast Track | Know the System |
| Personal Selection | Teamwork |
| Fit the Human Resources Profile (Text Book) | Roles/Responsibilities |
| Liked by Management | People Respect Them |
| Look Like Me | Look Like System |
| Make Good Presentations | Fact Management |
| Talk the Talk | Walk the Talk |
| Action Oriented (Reactive) | Proactive Plan Orientated |
| Boss or Chair Person | BSC and Visual Management |
| Tells you they are the best | Shows they are the best |
| Evaluation Based on Old System (Not System Values) | People Know Who THEY Are |
| They Manage the System | System Manages Them |
| Culture Changes Based on Leader | Culture Lives. Continuous Improvement exists. |
| Firm gets bought— name changes. | Firm survives. Everyone knows who they are. Everyone wants to copy. |

**Figure 3.1**

Do an assessment. Do these people listen? Do they understand the standards? Can they be coached? Do others respect them, including their peers, people who report to them, and others? Do they accomplish work based on being reactive, or are they proactive? Does their management style rely on pretty presentations, or do they use fact management and keep communication clear and focused?

## CIP Team Size

The size of the CIP team must be proportionate to the organization and the plan. The standard is typically one team member per 100 employees, but the leader and sensei have to apply due diligence, logistics, and the curve to the standard to determine the best number and how best to achieve it.

The size of the team is based not only on the size of the organization but also on the current skills of the organization. The organization's skills are characterized by its level on the 3Gs—how well executives do the "go and sees."

Due diligence includes understanding the effectiveness of current tools such as quality circles, Lean efforts, and idea systems. Some organizations may have Lean tools functioning in one area and the culture working in another. It's the responsibility of the sensei to do his or her due diligence in determining the current state of the organization's transformation and the best size of the team.

Having 10% of the organization on this team doesn't mean all these people are dedicated to facilitating kaizen events or even coaching pilot halls around the organization. It doesn't even mean that they are all on one central improvement team. A team member may be an executive, the pilot hall leader, or someone dedicated to coaching and training the tools on the Transformation Curve. Most organizations cannot support massive, rapid change, nor should they, and having too many people on this team at the beginning will lead to more problems in the future.

## An Overview of the Continuous Improvement Program

The CIP starts with simple tools and then moves to more advanced tools, moving from simple improvements to daily living and linking other tools of the system. Figure 3.2 below includes individual suggestions, team suggestions, kaizen events, and quality control circles.

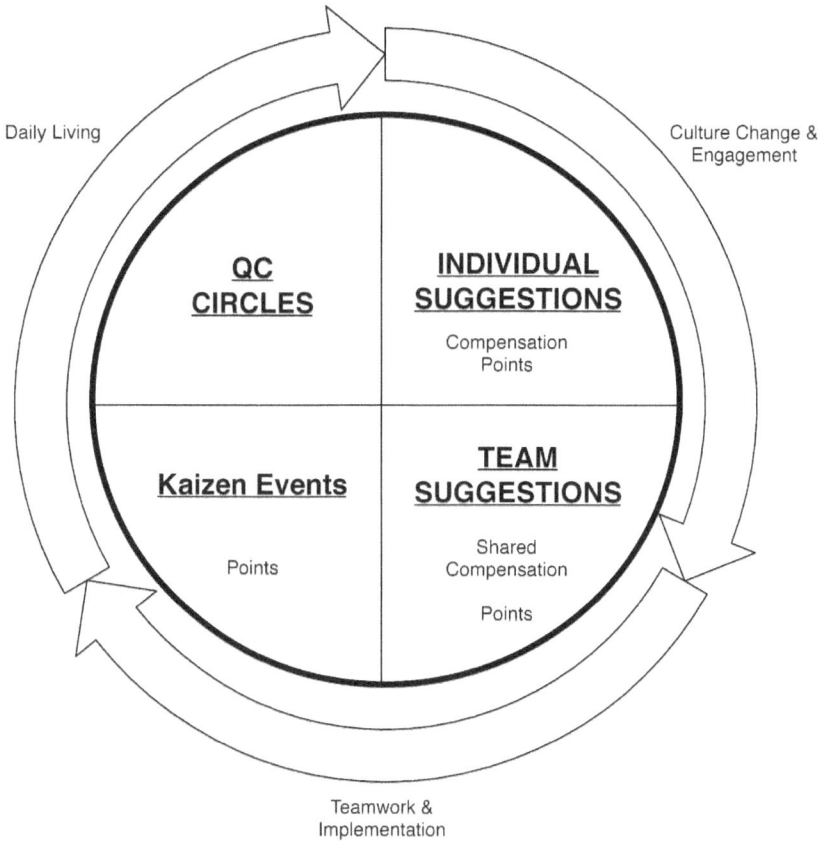

**Figure 3.2**

Generally, individual suggestions or improvements are introduced in Level A's improvement system, team suggestions in Level B's teamwork, kaizen events in Level C's meeting facilitation, and quality control circles in Level D. The Continuous Improvement Program aligns with the organizational strategy and includes compensation and the problem-solving system that aligns problem recognition with improvement. Grasping the CIP is the next step after top-level engagement so that this team can make a plan for how many improvements it may need, of what type, and where.

## Phase Three Target: A Mix of Improvements

In order for the Continuous Improvement Program to become world class, it must be linked with the rest of the system components and the strategic plan. If a target is to solve 1,000 problems a year, the proper mix of individual suggestions, 5 Whys, Fishbone diagrams, kaizen events, Six Sigma projects, and other problem-solving initiatives is needed to make this goal achievable.

In the Continuous Improvement Program, the components—individual suggestions, team suggestions, and introduction to kaizen and quality circles—are all linked and introduced strategically as the culture and a mindset focused on eliminating waste develop. The leader shouldn't just want 12,000 individual suggestions a year or 1,000 improvement projects a year. To become world class, the organization should start with simple tools, advancing to more and more complex tools but never letting go of the simple tools. When the full plan is working at world class, all the different types of problem solving and improvements are working. In world-class systems, 90% of the problems solved each day utilize the 5 Whys, and 90% of the suggestions the system creates are based on the 5 Whys. The other 10% are a mix of kaizen events and quality circles—larger-scale, generally proactive improvement projects.

Leaders must reinforce and try to employ all the tools within the organization. Many leaders who don't use the Transformation Curve but claim to use Lean say, "Oh, we have to do all these complex Six Sigma projects and kaizen events to solve our complex problems."

Though these organizations do use large Six Sigma teams and kaizen teams to solve problems, the rest of the organization fails to improve while waiting for the "problem solvers" to arrive. This reflects the culture, and when teams go into kaizen events, the results typically aren't sustained because the rest of the system isn't in place to support them and other people are not empowered or engaged in the process on a daily basis.

## Rewards and Compensation

The Continuous Improvement Program utilizes both rewards and recognition. Generally, the individual suggestion system offers a fixed reward for every implemented improvement. With team suggestions, that same fixed reward is split by the team. Per the policy, every individual or team suggestion receives a reward of $25 or $50. Though financial incentives aren't the purpose of the system, the reward must be significant for individuals as well as teams. When the pilot and the organization add team suggestions to the policy from a team consisting of five individuals, a $5 or $10 reward violates mutual trust and respect because individuals perceive they are only valued at $1 or $2 per individual.

Also, every suggestion that is implemented receives the same reward, since the system doesn't revolve around cost savings but rather around supporting the balanced scorecard (safety, quality, etc.) and being creative, no matter the impact.

These suggestions are team member owned and implemented. This is a system, a mechanism, to harness and support employee creativity. Because employees help the organization succeed and profit, they are given more than just thanks; they are paid, and that payment becomes part of their overall compensation package linked to behaviors and the balanced scorecard. (With kaizen events and quality circles, there is no monetary compensation.)

## Planning for Payment

Every program in the Toyota Production System has to be paid for by eliminating waste. Rewards are monetary for individual and team suggestions, and the sensei and leader are responsible for determining how they will pay for the system by eliminating waste. For a suggestion system to be implemented that respects the organization and is kick-started without negativity from leadership and the supervisory board, the sensei and leader need to decide how to pay for the ideas.

Figuring out where the money will come from without implying the need to carve out a new budget line is the first step. Receiving one suggestion per employee, with 1,000 employees, makes 1,000 suggestions in the first year or two feasible. That means that in five years, there will be 5,000 to 6,000 suggestions. The sensei/leader who plans to pay $50 per implemented suggestion must know where to eliminate waste in order to pay for the improvement/suggestion system. Eventually (from year two onward), the suggestion system will pay for itself through the ideas and consequent waste elimination and link to the balanced scorecard. In the meantime, leaders can't say to a customer, "Give me $500,000 to help pay for the suggestion system."

Leaders must be able to link the strategy with the Continuous Improvement Program and then use the suggestion system to help achieve goals by empowering people. This gives team members tools to improve and eliminate waste with the appropriate support from leadership.

Again, it's the responsibility of the leader, with help from the sensei, to link the approval portion of the suggestion system to the waste portion and eliminate waste to pay for the improvement.

Many people miss these critical aspects. They think suggestions will eliminate waste; they don't realize people need to be focused and the pilot used to leverage waste elimination. The system balances the 3Gs and 3Ps and must be a part of a long-term strategic plan to become world class.

## The Points System

In addition to monetary rewards, points are given based on each suggestion's link to the balanced scorecard. For example, safety might receive five points, quality four points, and so on. Individual suggestions, team suggestions, and kaizen events are all given points. On a yearly basis (at minimum), the team members with the most points receive additional rewards/ recognition.

The points system is a way to reinforce the balanced scorecard (safety first) and to emphasize safety and quality suggestions over financially driven suggestions. No points are given for quality circles because they are a part of daily living and maintaining the system and are planned for proactively through the annual planning cycle.

Primarily, the points system is a way to introduce and maintain organizational flexibility to achieve a very focused target and align the annual planning theme to the suggestion system. For example, if a hospital identifies a certain type of infection as a top problem and needs the entire organization to respond quickly to implement suggestions, the number of points can be increased from four to ten. This will help team members focus on suggestions to reduce those infections more quickly than they would have otherwise.

This system costs nothing extra, though the executives must be sure to perform even more go-and-sees on those particular suggestions. Meanwhile, this top down, bottom up flexibility, aligned with organizational strategy and a new team structure, is an extremely powerful way for organizations to react to internal and external problems both proactively and reactively. Without the culture of daily suggestions in place, it isn't possible.

# The Individual Suggestion System, a Phase One Tool

Initially, introducing all the levels of the Continuous Improvement Program at the same time is unnecessary and counterproductive. The organization won't be able to support this, leaders won't be able to comprehend it, everyone will be confused, and it simply won't work.

Just like using the 5 Whys to teach the discipline of problem solving on a daily basis, the Continuous Improvement Program starts with simple individual suggestions. Too many organizations think they can start with kaizen events when the employees aren't engaging in simple improvements and leaders aren't recognizing positive behaviors to get more improvements and results. Starting with the individual suggestion system is critical and later will be linked to the problem-solving system and top problems to generate team improvements linked tightly to the balanced scorecard. Kaizen events will be a natural part of the organization, organizing multifunctional teams to solve problems supported and maintained by the rest of the system.

## Purpose of the Suggestion System

The suggestion system has three purposes. First, it is a system to recognize good behavior and positive improvement. Second, it gives executives and leaders the opportunity to see and learn in a positive atmosphere. Third, it eliminates waste.

In essence, a suggestion system is a learning process, a doing process, and a waste elimination process. It focuses on creating an elimination of waste mindset in team members and creating a positive, action-oriented organization in which everyone can contribute to making work better.

## Individual Suggestions

Generally, leaders can't have face-to-face discussions with team members in line, because that would circumvent the supervisor and violate mutual trust and respect. Additionally, it would stop the team member from creating value—i.e. doing their daily work.

Leaders must use the suggestion system as a way to see and touch everyone—the mass of the organization. This mass is where the bulk of change is needed to shift the culture, with leadership following. Changing the mass is done by going, seeing, learning, rewarding, and recognizing. The suggestion system is the best system for ensuring this happens, and leaders must be sure to perform many go and sees, using the suggestion system as the framework to contact team members when they do good things, reinforcing the positive.

## Go, See, Recognize, Learn

The sensei and leader need to go and see as many implemented suggestions as possible to interact with the people who are making the suggestions. This is primarily to recognize people and also to learn from those who are doing the actual work of the organization. Seeing and touching suggestions gives leaders the opportunity to see something in or around the implemented idea and to suggest other opportunities for improvement. Seeing every suggestion allows leaders to help adapt, standardize, and make resources available to deploy the suggestion throughout the organization. Of course, organic communication across people and departments is always better than a leader deciding, but within every implemented suggestion, there are many more ideas than the leader can help unlock.

## Tiered Celebrations

Team members are recognized daily for their suggestions, with monthly recognition within departments and across organizations for the most creative or innovative suggestions. There are then quarterly recognitions, with the opportunity to be recognized as having contributed the best suggestion of the year in a given department. These lead to the past year's winners deciding the top three suggestions of the year. The suggestion boards that show monthly, quarterly, and annual winners help promote the culture and recognize the most impactful suggestions. These suggestions also become an artifact in the system for leaders to reference regarding whom to go and see, especially in larger organizations in which the CEO cannot be in every department frequently.

Each yearly winner (for most creative/innovative suggestion) receives his or her reward of $50, $100, $500, or whatever the policy/standard dictates. Then the organization's annual top ten suggestions each get their rewards, and then the top three. From the top three, the suggestion that best represents the organization becomes winner of the year. Both the most creative/innovative suggestions and those that get the most points should be rewarded equally.

Though the compensation is linked to the organizational strategy, the celebration is really a way to recognize team members for their efforts, to perpetuate the system, and to continually build momentum, focusing on the positive throughout the organization. Monetary compensation promotes mutual trust and respect between individuals and the organization. When people begin to see the monthly, quarterly, and yearly winners, they will want to be winners too, and the quality and number of suggestions will continue to increase.

## Recognition Yields More Improvements

When a leader wants to discuss a suggestion with the person who initiated the idea, s/he should never interrupt this team member's standard work. Instead, the company leader should ask the employee's team leader to temporarily step in and cover the work or have the team leader decide when an interruption might be appropriate. The daily meeting is a great time to recognize suggestions, as other team members see the recognition, thereby reinforcing the system. Regardless of when it takes place, the individual who makes the suggestion should be acknowledged, thanked, and rewarded, both monetarily and later with a personal touch.

Nearly every organization that has adapted TPS using the Transformation Curve pays for every suggestion. In addition, Rodger personally reaches out to each person through the candy he keeps in his pocket. Giving candy as a personal reward is an effective and inexpensive way for him to learn about and come in contact with people in the organization. It's exciting that people are paid for implementing ideas, but the addition of a company leader personally seeing the idea, saying thanks, and handing over a small personal gift is an excellent motivator. Rodger has had people ask him to come and see their improvement and then ask him for candy. Everyone knows that Rodger always has candy, but more importantly, they know he wants to learn about their suggestions.

At one point, the chairman of a company came with Rodger to reward and recognize improvement. Wearing safety shoes, safety glasses, and gloves, he spent the whole morning walking around the plant and looking at suggestions. Even with a language barrier (the employees spoke German, while the chairman spoke French), he understood the value of the suggestion system. Because the system promotes visual management (drawings, pictures, go and sees, etc.) and strong, clear communication between employees and their superiors, the chairman understood everything his team members told him. The system focuses on learning to see, while offering rewards helps get executives on the floor to see, reward, and recognize.

Going to learn about ideas for improvement, asking questions, being sincere, and thanking people is always much more meaningful than a monetary reward. However, the monetary reward helps promote mutual trust and respect. The team member is going above and beyond by helping the organization achieve goals through daily improvements. This will eventually impact the bottom line, and the employee should share in that benefit. Recognition without reward is not as powerful because it doesn't promote mutual trust and respect between the team member and the organization. Once people's hearts and minds are captured and they understand the essence of individual suggestions, team members can begin working together on team suggestions.

## TEAM SUGGESTIONS, KAIZEN EVENTS, AND QUALITY CONTROL CIRCLES

Team suggestions, kaizen events, and quality control circles become natural progressions of individual suggestions. Generally, team suggestions are introduced in Level B, kaizen events are introduced in Level C meeting facilitation, and quality control circles are introduced in Phase Three. Like every other tool, all are introduced and tested in the pilot hall first. Teamwork and team structure should be forming when introducing team suggestions. Figure 3.3 below shows the requirements along the CIP curve.

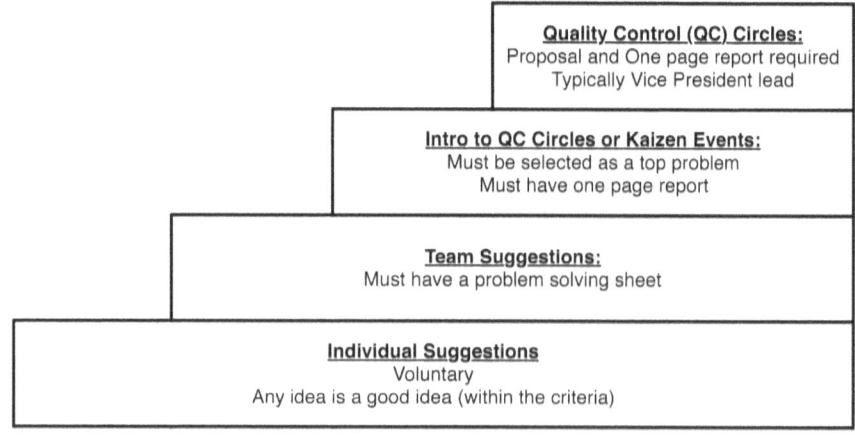

**Figure 3.3**

At all levels and stages of the Continuous Improvement Program, the individual suggestion system must be working very well. As the team and organization progress from individual to team, some level of problem solving one must in place and teamwork should be becoming the norm. The team structure may or may not be in place formally, but individuals are more helpful, responding to some strategic andons, and have proactive measures on the fourth row of the balanced scoreboard.

## Team Suggestions

Team suggestions within the Continuous Improvement Program are more structured than individual suggestions but are not as structured as a kaizen event or quality circle. The structure of a team links teamwork and problem solving. At a minimum, the team will use a problem-solving sheet and identify the problem statement, the 5 Whys, a root cause, the countermeasure, and employ a checking mechanism.

The team may or may not use the tools of a kaizen like a charter, one-page report, standard meeting agenda, etc., because often they are too complex. The compensation is the same for an individual suggestion as it is for a team suggestion, but the reward is split amongst the team.

Team suggestions are a great mechanism to begin introducing more advanced problem-solving tools as they become necessary. Mature team suggestions may use a one-page report to communicate the status or problem of a suggestion. Team suggestions are generally initiated by a team member or team leader, whereas kaizen events may be dictated or established from a top problem on the balanced scoreboard.

## Kaizen Events

Kaizen events, along with quality circles, become a progression to team suggestions, and teams will sustain and make further suggestions to support the work of a kaizen event. Because kaizen events take more time, resources, planning, and follow-up than individual and team suggestions, they must be linked to a top problem either proactively or reactively on the balanced scoreboard. To allow a leader to randomly select a problem that needs to be solved and then initiate a kaizen event violates mutual trust and respect. If the problem isn't linked back to the team's or organization's balanced scorecard clearly, why spend the time and resources on it? When scorecards and the culture are in place, kaizen events are great ways to achieve results, redesign work, and engage teams in improvement.

Kaizen events are generally introduced in the pilot hall once the team structure is in place, team suggestions are working, and there are a multitude of proactive key performance indicators on the scoreboard. These events may be used case by case to solve an operational problem that needs to be fixed immediately but won't necessarily immediately become part of the culture.

In terms of the overall Continuous Improvement Program, there is no payment for kaizen events, but there are points. Those who participate in a kaizen event linked to safety receive the same number of points as a person who implements a safety improvement. Kaizen events are linked to other Level C tools such as meeting facilitation, effective listening, and standard work one.

In terms of leading and facilitating, the CIP team may help facilitate a kaizen event, but it is expected that individuals are either in the process of learning a new tool themselves or teaching the leader of the area how to use a tool. This team shouldn't be running all over the organization facilitating and keeping track of events.

Some companies develop kaizen event promotion offices to monitor and track kaizen events in an attempt to hit a yearly number. Though a target number of improvements may be set at the beginning of the year (a mix of the entire Continuous Improvement Program), planning proactively for teams to solve problems is more important than hitting a specific number of events. If the output of the events isn't linked to the rest of the system in leadership and daily behavior, conducting a kaizen event is merely a problem-solving activity that most likely will not be sustained.

## QUALITY CONTROL CIRCLES

Quality control circles are led by the vice president and typically involve a proposal, last six to twelve months, and highlight several "events" to achieve the end results. Quality circles are proactive in nature and begin to manage a very small gray zone. They come out of the annual planning cycle, with the vice presidents setting a goal to lead a certain number of quality control circles in a year—usually two, even when the system is mature.

Before introducing quality control circles, the rest of the system must be established, including a proposal, a master plan, planned checkpoints, and proactive indicators. If there isn't a robust annual planning cycle, if teams aren't engaged in daily improvements, or if maintenance of the system and processes isn't established, a quality control circle will not be as effective and can even harm the organization. The quality control circle must improve results proactively. More importantly, it must not let earlier improvements slip through the cracks. No points or monetary rewards are given for participating in quality control circles because they are part of the culture, are mandatory to protect one's job, and are linked to the organizational compensation strategy.

## Sustaining the Suggestion System

Sustaining the suggestion system is a baseline for employment, meaning everyone has roles and responsibilities within the suggestion system, whether hourly, technical, or management. The system becomes the standard, and suggestions are the driver. This ensures continuous improvement stability.

A company may receive 10,000 to 12,000 suggestions annually, or ten per employee implemented. Some workforces implement 10-, 15-, or 20,000 suggestions a year, and the leader just passes out candy and $50 rewards. Quickly, the system begins to work, and the leader gets the very fun job of rewarding, recognizing, and encouraging further improvement. In Phases 2 and 3, through the annual planning cycle, leaders must determine goals—how many suggestions, team improvements, and problems they want solved each year. The majority of problems solved should be simple problems using the suggestion system and 5 Whys. The leader must focus on simple improvements and ultimately needs to decide if a kaizen event is necessary based on top problem selection and the annual planning cycle.

If leaders only promote kaizen events and don't reinforce the simple improvements through go and sees, rewards, and recognition, people will not be inspired to use the kaizen event and the system will not support the improvements.

To clarify, in the beginning, suggestions may affect all kinds of things and may be scattered across all areas of the organization because, in this phase, the focus is on creativity. But at Toyota, team members do not affect any change that affects the standard. Changes to standards cannot be implemented unless they are proven positive changes. If they affect the standard (safety, quality, productivity, or inventory) or are cost driven, the team member and team leader need to make sure they fit within the standard, the balanced scorecard, and the strategic plan.

At Toyota, the balanced scorecard is linked to improvement, especially to changes in standards. A team member can't simply say, "I'm going to implement something." In the daily living phase, improvements are very tightly linked to standard work and the rest of the system.

## Linking World-Class Behaviors and the CIP

Leaders aim to ensure that each employee is on a quality circle or kaizen event team. If team members don't participate in team suggestions by collecting data, recording, doing prep, or so on, they can't work at the organization. All of the components of the Continuous Improvement Program—individual, team, kaizen, quality control circles—are necessary, and people must participate in team-based improvement activities. If team members do not want to support improvement, they are essentially saying they do not want to work at the organization. Individual suggestions aren't mandatory, but team members must participate in team suggestions and improvements. People who aren't able to do so will leave because they do not fit within the system and the new desired culture.

Simply put, the system hires, trains, and terminates people—individuals within the system do not. On the positive side, people who want to make improvements and want to be involved in team suggestions, kaizen, and quality circles will be drawn to the organization, and the culture will be perpetuated. During the hiring process, the focus will be on identifying people who fit the organization's culture, and many individuals will aspire to be involved in making improvements.

## Executive Learning

In Phase One especially, many executives do not see and understand the full power of the suggestion system because they focus on one suggestion, one improvement. Many try to calculate the cost savings and bottom line impact of that one improvement, but this is usually impossible and quite frankly is a waste of time. The suggestion system is just that—a system—and the power of the system and all the components working together (go and sees, reward, recognition, etc.) creates the culture, reinforcing the positive and encouraging more improvements.

## *Who Coaches Whom?*

The sensei must be mindful of who is coaching whom, keeping in mind that it's critical for executive leaders to work from the top and bottom.

Generally speaking, it doesn't work for executive leaders to be coached or instructed by CIP members. Executives don't want low-level employees telling them about their bad behaviors and what they should be doing. For this reason, expecting the chairman or president to sit down with the CIP team isn't as effective as it needs to be, especially during the cultural change phase.

Until the CIP process is functional, with the president or vice president on a kaizen team and the team leader acting as a team member, the organization needs a sensei to coach the executive leader.

## *Executives Must Show Respect*

A great story of a fantastic suggestion and executive learning took place in the final product testing area of one company shortly after it started implementing the Transformation Curve's suggestion system, when a team member suggested color coding the cable system so he'd know exactly where the cables went without having to look at the ends to see what they looked like.

This was a very simple yet potentially highly impactful suggestion, since putting the wrong cable on the electrical that went on the fuel could cause a fire. The team member was very proud of the suggestion, and so was Rodger, given its focus on safety.

When two executives snickered about this suggestion, Rodger asked them to stay the rest of the day and make two suggestions to improve the process. This was a great opportunity to demonstrate, "If you're going to laugh, you get to stay and make an improvement." This was a learning experience for these executives, and it was the sensei's job to help them learn by recognizing positive behaviors and/or using the positive as a means to overcome the negative.

## *Executives Must Lead*

Positivity and simplicity are important for executives to learn, as is encouraging or suggesting further improvements when possible.

One chief executive went to see his first suggestions and started explaining to team members why he and his team were visiting, emphasizing that all suggestions mattered, even the small, seemingly insignificant ones.

Oddly enough, this comment may have been taken the wrong way, because to those team members, every suggestion was meaningful and impactful, especially at the onset of the system.

Another executive saw a suggestion and asked the team member, "Is this in every other department? What do we need to do to get this in every other department?"

The team member was confused—how could she possibly implement her idea in every department when she only worked in one?

Questions about standardization and deployment throughout the organization or similar departments need to be directed to team leaders and supervisors, not team members. After performing go-and-sees, learning, and coaching further suggestions, executives must perform Plan-Do-Check-Act and reflect on what they've learned and how they can help perpetuate the culture and coach through direct reports.

Using the balanced scorecard, giving points and recognition, coaching the system, and going and seeing drive cultural change and maintain the gains to become world class. Leaders and executives must especially manage the 3Ps and the 3Gs with individual suggestions.

In sum, in the Continuous Improvement Program, teamwork is mandatory. If team members or executive leaders can't support the standards of improvement, they can't work at the organization. The system hires and promotes people, and by and large it creates a culture that helps the organization hire the right people, while the people who fit in culturally want to work for the organization.

# Chapter 4

# The Pilot Area— Coaching and Tools

At Toyota, Rodger was standing in the middle of the plant, learning to see. Learning to see the good, learning to see the variance, and learning to see the standard. He was learning to see what he needed to focus on from a behaviors, tools, and coaching standpoint in order to achieve the goal.

Most leaders are not able to do this, because learning to see is very difficult and many times happens slowly. Executives who "stand in the circle" too early will only see the negative—they will see people rather than processes making errors.

From a transformation perspective, leaders can learn to see and learn how to behave much more quickly in a focused area with all the tools working than they can from any other place in the organization. Therefore, a pilot area or frontline area focused on the tools and behaviors of the Transformation Curve is chosen to help executives learn how to behave and to show the organization the success of the system.

To move too quickly throughout the organization without a mature pilot is a mistake. As coaches in the system, leaders cannot move too quickly or be expected to have too many Plan-Do-Check-Act (PDCA) cycles. If they have too many balanced scorecards or too many key performance indicators, they can't coach—they can't exhibit all the behaviors all the time that are necessary to create and sustain change.

If leaders can't touch and coach around their balanced scorecards, people will feel like they aren't getting recognition, and the engagement needed between leaders and teams to drive the fourth row will be missing. Therefore, asking every department to start balanced scorecards is not the key. Simply having hourly PDCA without the right information going to the right person at the right time is not helpful.

Leaders are better off starting slowly, selecting proactive key performance indicators linked to the six-year balanced scorecard—both at the executive and pilot levels—and providing positive recognition to the teams that drive the results. Starting out too fast and then realizing the leader can't support and manage the process can cause the team or organization to backslide.

In short, leaders must focus on the areas that can help impact the long-term strategic plan first. They must start where the most benefit can occur from a behavior and performance standpoint. That is the essence of the pilot hall. It's not the number of areas or the number of balanced scorecards that matters; it's the results, and their consequent impact on safety, quality, and developing people to become future senseis.

## Becoming Proactive

The balanced scorecard and the checks that support it must move the organization toward its goal without creating more waste. Leaders should not say, "We must have 5,000 scorecards" or "We must have 100 balanced scorecards," because the organization won't be able to plan or budget for that.

Essentially, having a balanced scorecard also means having a daily meeting, metrics, indicators, top problems, and the accompanying supporting tools. This takes an hour a day, or a half hour to support and a half hour to go and see.

Perhaps the leader invites 10 people to a daily meeting that lasts 45 minutes. If none of the other tools are working to support the daily meeting—there is no problem solving, no suggestions, no balanced scorecard with proactive fourth row measures—the meeting won't accomplish much. If everybody in the plant is in an hour-long huddle and 80% of them are thinking about their next break, 15% are passively engaged, and 5% are doing the work, how will this create value for the organization?

Instead, the daily meeting, monthly meetings, quarterly reviews, and eventually hourly checks should not be wasteful; they should be proactive checks.

By eliminating waste, space is made to hold these meetings, and the time is compensated for. The organization improves. The PDCA cycle checks pay for themselves in waste elimination.

This is akin to giving employees eight hours to complete a task and paying them for eight hours regardless of how long it takes. If they can eliminate waste and complete the task in seven hours, they will have an hour to problem solve, create suggestions, or do what's needed to improve for next month. By eliminating waste, more value can be created. With more value, more waste can be eliminated, leaving more time for improvements.

The individual suggestion system helps link the top down, bottom up approach from an engagement and daily improvement perspective, but alone it's not enough. In order to learn how to lead from the middle and support the top down, bottom up strategy, a pilot area is selected so that leaders can implement many of the Phase One tools at the executive level and coach/support all of the Phase One tools at the pilot level. The Continuous Improvement Program (CIP) creates an initial systematic link between the top and bottom of the organization.

From this pilot area, leaders can coach, lead, and support transformation. This helps executives and the organization see the tools working at the top and the bottom of the organization, together driving results and behaviors.

Aligning behaviors to strategy is very important for top down implementation and bottom up support, but most organizations don't have this. Instead, their leaders think, "You people should do a kaizen event and problem solving."

They don't ask, "How do I, as a leader, move up and down through the organization to achieve our goals?"

Leaders must be able to problem solve as team members, both on the line and in kaizen teams. They must grasp the behaviors and skills necessary to become world class. If they rely on top-down command and control, they will never harness the energy and skill set of the entire organization.

# The Pilot Hall Area— Where Tools and Behaviors Are Linked

The pilot hall or pilot area is a focused, frontline group within the organization chosen to use the Toyota Production System (TPS) and to learn and introduce more advanced tools.

In the beginning, the pilot serves many purposes—it's a vision of what the organization will look like, a place to train people, and a place to test/implement new tools, going deep into the Transformation Curve.

The pilot organically transforms from a frontline area where others can see TPS in action to a place where leaders learn problem solving to a place where the organization learns, does research, and tests large-scale improvements. It can also become a space where new processes/products are introduced and linked to the strategy and business case of the organization. Eventually, when the system (Levels A through C) is functioning, it becomes a place for innovation.

In order to be successful, the pilot hall must reflect all of Phase One (Levels A and B) and part of Phase Two (Level C). An important goal is to be able to see all the tools linked and in action and to grasp their impact.

Subsequently, when others see the pilot, they not only see the tools but also hear about their benefits. Together, the leader and sensei strive to get tools working in the pilot linked to the organization's structure—one team leader for five team members. During the first few years, the pilot demonstrates Levels A, B, and parts of C so that people can see what the organization will look like in five years and can then adapt and apply these tools to their specific areas.

The pilot is also the place to infiltrate new business, products, or services into the system. Say a new tool goes into production and causes a disturbance to the value stream. It will then be passed to the customer, which means the people and the organization will pay for it.

The pilot is a buffer to plan for the new tool. For example, when the pilot is ready for an andon system, it may build ahead, knowing that tomorrow there may be more disturbances in the process caused by andon.

The pilot is also the place where the sensei and leader can introduce quality circles, kaizen events, team suggestions, uniforms—all the tools of Level A through C and the rest of the Transformation Curve. Generally, the sensei and leader can introduce the manager of the pilot hall to the tool, and s/he can coach everyone else. Then, those people who understand the tool and align with the culture can be integrated into the rest of the organization by moving into the next pilot hall as team leaders.

Coaches create coaches, and eventually the CIP team may consist only of a few full-time people because everyone is essentially a continuous improvement person. Eventually, a leader will be able to go into the organization or team saying, "We need to do a quality circle focused on this problem. Who wants to participate?"

People will be actively engaged, and it won't have to be scheduled in advance. Improvement time will be built into the schedule, and needed improvements will be made because individuals follow the standard process of a quality circle.

Thus, the organization ends up with thousands of kaizen people instead of the traditional few in a Six Sigma team or kaizen promotion office. Eventually, everyone will know and use the system, but they will learn it in the pilot.

## Choosing the Pilot Area

The pilot area must be chosen based on which area will:

- Have the highest safety, quality, productivity, human development, and cost benefits
- Achieve the most benefit from other people seeing the system working
- Develop people to continue spreading the system

A pilot shouldn't be chosen based on a successful leader or in an attempt to prop up a failing leader. It must be linked to the strategy and the executive team, and the executive leader and sensei must be able to ensure the pilot's success.

One organization may need a pilot to show success in finance, another in satisfaction, and another in culture. It's all based on the due diligence the sensei does prior to suggesting, selecting, and starting the pilot.

From a strategic standpoint, the pilot may be chosen from within the realm of finance, culture, or a mix of both, depending on the current state of the human/operations balance of the organization. If the company is making money and is financially sound, the pilot may be chosen from a cultural standpoint. If the company isn't making money, pilot selection may be financially driven. If it's culturally driven, that should be communicated to the entire organization.

However, if the pilot is financially driven, the sensei and leader can't charge in and start screaming that the system is about making money. The purpose of a financially driven pilot may not necessarily be to make money but rather to show that the system and the culture work, with being profitable a positive byproduct. That helps other leaders, the board, or shareholders in some cases get excited about the system and recognize the success of the pilot. In other words, the pilot needs to be a place where the sensei can expose the rest of the organization to the system, the expected behaviors that drive culture, and the operational results.

One organization that produced products that were sold long-term to the government chose a pilot based solely on culture. Products weren't built and shipped to customers frequently, so it was hard to show the success of the system from a quality and customer standpoint. A different pilot had to be chosen in order to show more frequent success and to demonstrate that the system worked. In this case, focusing on culture was the right decision.

Some healthcare organizations choose pilots for the wrong reasons. One hospital chose the laboratory as a pilot because that's where it thought "the tools" applied best, since labs are similar to production lines and concepts like a U-shape cell, andon, 5S, and other tools could be applied. But from a customer/patient standpoint, what benefit did this bring to patients that could be seen and felt? What benefit did it bring to the insurance companies paying the bills?

True, a pilot can be selected because it resembles manufacturing, but TPS isn't about manufacturing. It's about developing people, standardizing processes, and creating a culture of improvement. Therefore, the pilot must be chosen based on the impact to the strategy and the culture of the organization—it's not just about seeing the tools working. The pilot must be linked to the strategy and positively impact the customer in a noticeable way, which means it is linked to results.

## Level A in the Pilot

The pilot must incorporate all the tools and activities of Level A starting with the initial tools for top-level engagement. These tools include a balanced scorecard (six-year plan and visual scoreboard), a daily meeting, problem solving one, and annual/master plans along with the suggestion system, audits, checks, and leaders engaging with frontline staff to improve.

The pilot must also employ a master plan and adjust the plan based on problems, since master planning is not just for executives but is for everyone. The pilot must link top problems and the master plan, develop standard processes based on problem-solving countermeasures, and create visual management. Soon, the master plan will become proactive; top 3s and the proactive plan will be very similar.

The pilot must have a functioning 5S system to solve simple organizational problems. It must also have a safety system linked to the 5S system consisting of safety audits, the green cross to visualize safety, safety policy, and problem-solving standards linked to safety.

Culturally, teams must be willing to make changes within their own work and their own departments as evidenced by a large number of improvements and an increasing participation rate in the improvement system. Root cause analysis—mainly the 5 Whys—must be strong both in the pilot and within leadership supporting the pilot.

At a minimum, the CIP team must be experts in Level A and learning Level B within their own processes. Under the best circumstances, the system will create a pull for Level B tools. In other cases, the continuous improvement team can begin to lead the team towards Level B tools such as kanban one and andon one.

## Linking Levels A and B in the Pilot

The tools of Level B must be tested both in the pilot and with the executive team. These tools include teamwork, kanban one, andon one, and problem solving two. The purpose of Level B is to move from individual capability to team capability. The foundation of Level B is the management cycle, which links all the tools and incorporates them into daily living, performance evaluation, and team evaluation, but as explained earlier, because laying the foundation first is critical, the management cycle is not discussed in this book.

If the pilot team and executives don't understand the basics of the 5 Whys, it will be difficult to manage andons in Phase One. If they don't understand the basics of 5S, it will be difficult to maintain a kanban system. If the pilot team doesn't embrace and own improvement, with the executive team rewarding, recognizing, and advancing improvement while learning themselves, it will be very difficult to get the support and follow-through necessary to solve more advanced problems in a team setting. The visual of Level B of the Transformation Curve is shown in Figure 4.1.

### *Teamwork*

The tools of Level A are generally in place to help teamwork within the pilot hall become a reality on both the human and operational sides. Initially, this means focusing on the right metrics, using problem solving to solve problems, implementing improvements within the team's span of control, creating standards to support the process, and in general working more cohesively. The system helps build teamwork by changing the culture and outlook on problems. Once that individual culture begins to change, other people will embrace and lead change. Once the right PDCA, visual management, and roles/responsibilities are in place to support change, the pilot is probably ready to move into teamwork.

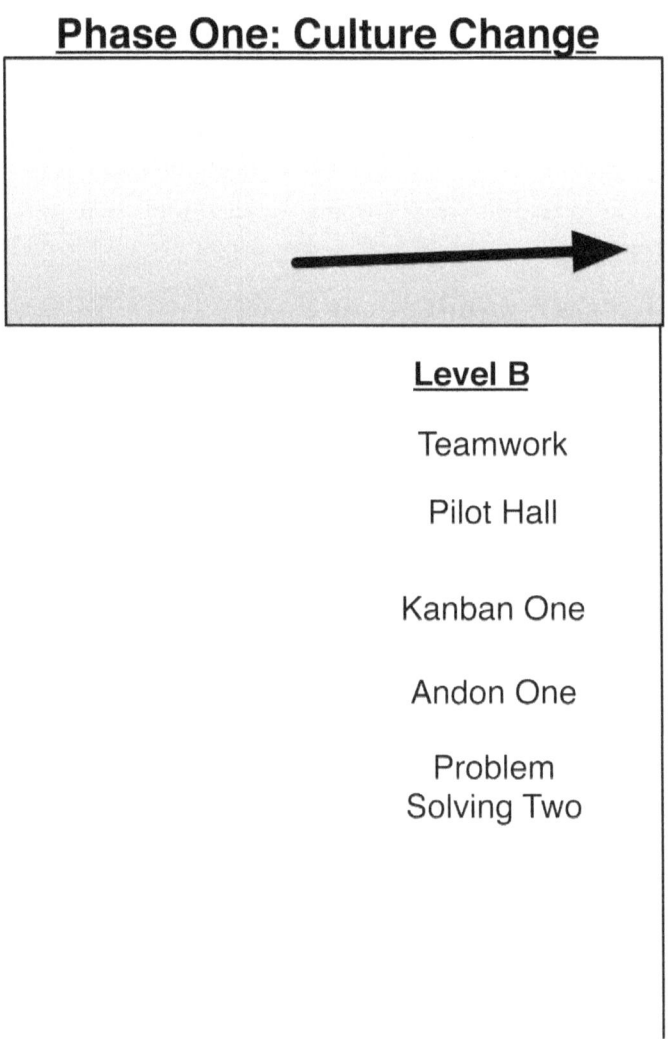

Figure 4.1

# The Pilot Area—Coaching and Tools

**Linking Other Teams.** A team is based upon teamwork, with quality, maintenance, production control, and finance key functions integrated into the pilot. The pilot and the teams integrated into the pilot need to work on cross-functional teams to support the pilot as well as the teams above, below, and side to side. The balanced scorecards must be linked to support the overlap as all teams strive toward the same world-class goals while working in tandem. It's everybody's job to share in teamwork, support the plan, and achieve the goals.

For example, if a problem-solving sheet arises that is Quality's responsibility, Production may be a part of the team to support the root cause analysis and countermeasures. If an inpatient unit and the emergency department are linked, targets on the balanced scorecard should include each team supporting each other. Surely, with active teamwork, the inpatient balanced scorecard won't be all green if the emergency department is drowning in red. The essence of teamwork is to find the best way to support the teams above, below, and to each side of one's own.

The teamwork model as shown in Figure 4.2 below is a visual representation of how a team overlaps with the teams above, below, and to each side. Improvement and daily work don't focus on doing one's own job the most efficiently and effectively but rather on "How does my work impact the teams around me?"

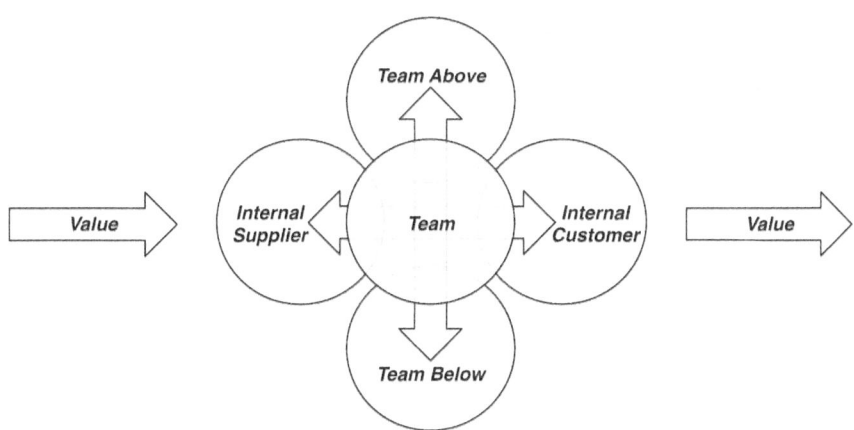

**Figure 4.2**

This model teaches individuals to value team thinking and redesigning work based on the entire process, not just one piece of it. Leaders need to know how to manage the overlap of each team to support the process. Though this concept is introduced to the executive team early on, it's put into action in the pilot in Level B. Later, the teamwork concept is used with the leadership model in teaching and embedding the management cycle. It is put into practice when designing organizational and team strategies that encourage team members to be cross trained and multifunctional—learning all the jobs within the overlaps. Tools like kanban one, andon one, and problem solving two help teams manage the overlaps.

**Team Structure.** Creating an organization to sustain TPS is not about building hierarchies or pyramids; it's about building teamwork that supports the teams below, above, and side to side. The more complex the organizational structure, the harder it is to maintain and support teamwork and achieve the balanced scorecard.

Within Phase Two, the culture is generally embedded—it's already in the hearts and minds of everybody. The organization is now hiring for culture, and there's a long-term strategic plan in place for organizational strategy, including the organizational structure.

This structure reflects the 1:5 system of team leader/member ratio. There is one group leader per group and five team leaders total; 1:5 supervisors, managers, and vice presidents. If an organization or facility has five vice presidents, it gets one executive vice president; that's the standard. Within support areas, the indirect ratio is 1:7 or 1:8 depending on the plan.

The goal of andon as it relates to team structure is to be multifunctional and flexible enough to put the andon in place so the patient doesn't suffer and the process doesn't stop. The system needs to be based on developing a flexible workforce and standards so that anyone can do them, which reduces cost and increases the knowledge base of work members.

It's not about putting a help chain in place to notify the president or CEO of a problem that needs solving. Andons are proactive, and the organizational structure supports proactive problem solving using andons.

Using the 1:5 team structure, team members will support teamwork and maintain the system. This means they may spend time on the line covering for vacations, conducting training for team members, responding to andons, checking data, doing safety checks, making sure material kanbans are flowing, and other necessary checks derived from problem-solving sheets, improvements, and the balanced scorecard. The target is for all team members in the pilot to become multifunctional and cross trained so that any of them can step in and respond to andon and work any position on the line. It can't just happen overnight, though; it must be planned and tested in the pilot.

**Monthly Master Plans.** As annual planning cycles become more robust and the team using the annual plans becomes more cohesive, the sensei may introduce monthly master plans. These plans are a way to link annual plans, top problems, and daily countermeasures identified through problem-solving sheets and suggestions that may need to be standardized. Monthly master planning will eventually be a tool for all leaders, but as the skill is developed, it should be used by each executive or vice president as well as the pilot hall leader(s).

As problems become more evident, longer-term countermeasures become necessary based on top problems. As suggestions are spread and kaizen activities are implemented, the content of the annual plans will become a tool to link daily problem solving with annual planning, both proactive and reactive. If a problem can't be solved within a standard time frame (48 hours), it needs to go on a master plan. The check cycle must be in place to help leaders. The art of planning, delegation, and control using tools like the monthly master plan will be integrated when the management cycle, a foundation of the system, is introduced and linked to performance evaluations.

*KANBAN ONE*

The pilot is where the organization learns about kanbans. To begin, start with the simple kanban such as a two-bin system on small parts and just-in-time kanban on big parts in the pilot hall. Whatever supplies, materials, and products the pilot is using should be on a kanban as quickly as possible (though not circumventing Level A).

In the healthcare industry, that means consumable patient supplies may be on a two-bin system, and the patient coming from one unit to the next (from the emergency department to the operating room, for example) may be on a kanban in a sense, being pulled to and from the pilot hall. An administrative area with papers, pencils, and reports should all be on kanban.

After the standard is established, the andons are set up to link to the kanban system. The new standard now stipulates that nothing moves in the pilot hall unless it's on the kanban—no product, no material, no service. That's what it will look like in five years throughout the organization and supplier/customer chain.

## Andon One

First and foremost, note that an andon doesn't stop the process—it keeps the process going. It's proactive, just like the fourth row of the balanced scoreboard. Andons are in place to ensure one-piece flow is delivered and to call for help using the 1:5 team structure.

Many people don't grasp the true essence of andons. Early on, when observing Toyota, andons were misinterpreted as an opportunity to stop the line for quality purposes. Some people still believe that stopping the line and andons are synonymous, but they aren't. The help chain is built into andons to call for help proactively, not reactively.

At Toyota, Rodger and the team knew exactly how many andon pulls would occur each day. The whole system was based on that standard, and the goal was to maintain it. From a high level, an "andon pull" doesn't necessarily mean there is a problem that must be solved; the pulls are built into the process based on capability studies.

However, andon pulls can't be incorporated without simple teamwork existing in the culture. If the simple 5 Whys aren't ingrained in the mentality of leadership and team members, leaders will respond to andons reactively and view the andon pull as a people problem, not a process problem.

Whether it's manufacturing, medical, or service, the system will identify who is having trouble with the process and who is about to experience a problem with safety, quality, productivity, etc. Andons establish a mechanism to support that part of the team and to keep the process going.

Andons don't have to incorporate a big visual board with audible signals; they should be kept simple, especially in andon one within the pilot. At one organization in Europe, the andon signal was a popular comedy movie's theme song, an audible signal that told a specific supervisor to look at a visual board to determine where to respond to an andon pull. When the song began, he had to be at a specific location within a specific amount of time. If he couldn't solve the problem within the timeframe, another audible signal would sound. The leader of his/her team would then know to respond to support the process.

Also, it's not always a leader who responds to an andon; it might be a quality specialist, someone in engineering, etc. The purpose isn't to command and control but rather to have people present who can support the process just in time. Too many organizations trying to implement the tool say, "If there's a problem that can't be solved, the CEO gets a call within 90 minutes." In some cases, that can be effective, but it tends to be a mechanism for command and control rather than a system linked to the annual plan, proactive problem solving, and teamwork.

## PROBLEM SOLVING TWO

Problem solving two consists of finding multiple causation points for a single point of recognition, i.e., solving many problems at one time. It builds on problem solving one, articulating a clear problem statement, using the 5 Whys to determine the root cause, and planning for countermeasures.

Teamwork is necessary in problem solving two. This tool doesn't necessarily require the 1:5 team structure but rather a teamwork mentality. If individuals focus on people, don't practice the 5 Whys daily, or aren't eager to support interlinked teams, it will be very difficult to identify true root causes of problems and to implement countermeasures that affect those root causes.

There may be multiple root causes within a long-term master plan that need to be tested and responded to with appropriate countermeasures. Additionally, proactive check cycles may be needed that link back to the fourth row of the balanced scorecard. The countermeasures may even be linked to a new andon. Without a functioning scoreboard and PDCA cycles around the scoreboard, proactive measures on the fourth row will be useless.

With the team structure in place, it is especially important at the beginning of Level B that a specialist, such as someone from quality or logistics or the continuous improvement team in Levels B or C, helps facilitate problem solving two in order to introduce it to the executive team and the pilot hall. Toyota had leaders facilitate problem-solving activities like kaizen events to develop this leader, who learned about the process and solved the problem.

Though it's not necessary to have the team structure fully deployed for problem solving two, team structure, especially the team leader relationship, helps to lead the charge. This is because problem solving two is more complicated than simple problem solving and often requires team members in one area or in a cross-functional team. Team structure and the appropriate team ratio frees up people to problem solve, with the team leader allowing team members to go when and where they are needed.

Many organizations use people on overtime as a problem-solving crutch when they don't have the team structure in place. When outsiders came to Toyota and observed problem solving two, kaizen events, and quality circles, they saw the improvement activity and its benefits, but they didn't realize the importance of daily problem solving, team structure, and the fact that the teams were already engaged in improvement, with the 5 Whys ingrained into daily behaviors and the organizational strategy as related to allowing people to solve problems in place.

To introduce kaizen events without the team structure might be possible, if there's enough overtime built into the budget, but overtime becomes waste and will impact the customer. Overtime means that improvement wasn't planned effectively organizationally or systematically. There must be an overall organizational plan for how many improvements are necessary—how many kaizen events, quality circles, and simple 5 Whys are necessary to achieve the annual plan. If the annual planning cycle isn't developed enough to plan for improvements, problem solving two is just another tool in the toolbox that isn't linked to the rest of the system.

The eventual goal is for teams to self-identify and lead the activity, after the standard for problem solving two and team problem solving has been adapted and developed within the organization, starting with the pilot.

Outside organizations sometimes assume this practice revolves around solving the problem and overlook the work leading to the problem-solving activity. They don't see the development plan for the leader, nor do they see the time spent during the activity integrated into the process time and the annual plan.

## Learning from the Pilot

In the past, some organizations sent people to Toyota to learn the system. These individuals learned the tools but not the interdependency of each tool. These leaders couldn't understand their roles and responsibilities and what to do if the tools weren't working—how to establish and pull the andon to get the tools to overlap and support the people and process.

The other mistake was in sending multiple people to Toyota for a year (usually not even at the same time). Then, instead of taking these people and putting them in one place to establish pilots for their organizations, they were sent to different places and told to "Implement TPS." Suffice it to say that this didn't work very well, and that's why the pilot is so important. It allows leaders to not only see the tools working but to link all the tools to create true teamwork.

Learning from world-class organizations is beneficial in seeing what not to do. However, it's very difficult to learn from world-class organizations how to adapt the system because it's too complex and advanced. The best learning is done in the pilot so that the system is adapted to the culture, the people, and the processes of the actual organization. A good sensei can coach the executives, the CIP team, and the pilot to create a model area to see the system working—Levels A, B, and parts of Level C—as quickly as possible.

To support this learning, leaders must communicate where the pilot hall is along with its objectives. Leaders must communicate clearly, "This is going to be a pilot hall where we train everybody and where we learn about the system. All leaders will go through the pilot hall, and executives are going to be working in the pilot hall."

*Don't Cast a Shadow*

The sensei's role in the pilot hall is to teach others and to ensure they learn the system properly. The sensei must not cast a shadow on the executive team, and neither the executive team, the CIP team, nor anyone else should cast a shadow on the pilot or any other part of the organization.

Casting a shadow can mean a number of things, but primarily it alludes to an individual taking credit when the credit needs to be given to the systematic approach. Casting a shadow also implies bringing inappropriate or negative attention to an individual or team. The sensei or coach must be able to make and facilitate change, with followers seeing the change come from the system and not individuals.

This may not be done through direct teaching but through observing, listening, and helping the leader/CIP team. The sensei needs to ensure that the designated coaches and leaders see what they need to see in the pilot, exhibit the behaviors required to help the pilot be successful, and understand when it is appropriate to use each tool. This is all done in a supportive way to help build mutual trust and respect between the organization, the pilot hall leader, the CIP team, and whatever internal coaches are dedicated to the system early on.

The sensei must make sure the leader is respected and that s/he, the sensei, doesn't cast a shadow. The sensei must likewise teach the leader not to cast a shadow on the continuous improvement team and back it up with coaching and clear standards for the system. If the leader or continuous improvement team member is embarrassed in the pilot or in front of a team, trust will be lost. It is the sensei's role—whether it's an internal or external sensei—to coach and ask the right questions in order to correct tactical mistakes and progress within the system at the most appropriate time.

Meanwhile, the continuous improvement team should always navigate to the standard. If this team doesn't know how to answer a question, it shouldn't simply offer an opinion. The standard has to be the basis for the answer because everyone needs to speak the same language and give the same feedback in order to be trusted and respected.

For this reason, mixing personal opinions into the system casts a shadow. In other words, the system can be adapted, but it cannot be personalized. The sensei must make sure all the coaches say the same thing at the same time. The focus is not on what they know or think they know; that will eventually confuse people with different answers and different standards. The CIP team's focus must be on maintaining the standards in place and learning the new standards. Team members may leave, leaders may leave, but the culture stays if the standards are put in place consistently and are independent of any given person. Likewise, if different standards and different interpretations of the standard exist, sharing, learning, and growing become much more difficult.

The sensei must go and see the pilots to check that internal coaches are teaching/ training/coaching people according to the standard. The sensei ensures that the standards, their application, and interpretation are clear; s/he also decides when it is time to change the standard or add to the standard knowledge and skill.

When introducing more advanced tools, movement isn't based on timing but on skill. From an application and behavior standpoint, the Continuous Improvement Program, pilot, and others must have the right skill level to move to the next tool and next concept. Typically, the pilot must be solidly into Level A before Level B is introduced.

# The Pilot Area—Coaching and Tools

## Don't Rush to Level B

Never introduce andons or kanbans until Level A is solidified. From a leadership standpoint, andons are meant to maintain the process, highlight problems, and anticipate fixing them. If leaders don't know how to engage in problem solving, if the process isn't standardized, if the team structure isn't in place, what good are andons?

Many organizations put andons in place and then scream, "This tool doesn't work!" They don't grasp the human structure that needs to be in place—the 1:5 team ratio—to support andon, total preventative maintenance, and the like. So the line actually does shut down or the tool just highlights problems without helping to solve them proactively.

Everything in the Transformation Curve is utilized strategically, at the appropriate time, because if the skill isn't matched with the right tool with the human infrastructure to support it, the tools won't work. In other words, it's about skill, not time—this tool is dependent on that one working, so if the first tool isn't working, there's no sense trying to get the next one to work.

More specifically, if the executive team isn't solving daily problems using simple 5 Whys very quickly, how can they be expected to implement the 5 Whys proactively when responding to an andon? Trying to use an andon system without the necessary support in place violates mutual trust and respect and will fail.

## Follow the Sequence

To emphasize this point, remember that trying to do andon one without Level A in place at the executive and pilot levels is like trying to race a motorcycle with no wheels. It can be done, but it's not going to work. If the problem-solving skill isn't embedded in the culture, if standards aren't established, there's no point in "implementing andon."

Leaders can't just read a book about andons without being engaged in daily problem solving (the simple 5 Whys) and having a master plan linked to the balanced scorecard. The key is to establish the roles and responsibilities that support the system. Leaders must know how to do PDCA and use its tools.

In the pilot, it's important to teach executives and leaders how to do simple 5 Whys, to link the process of the fourth row of the scoreboard to the andon system, to master the standard process, and to maintain the basic 5S with team leader checks to maintain the system and start proactively solving problems. Then, as the andon is advanced to other areas, it will be supported by the team structure of 1:5 throughout the organization; each person has the capacity and skill necessary for andon one to work.

Without these skills, neither the team nor the organization can be expected to solve problems immediately and proactively using andons because it's nearly impossible to implement an isolated tool without the sequence of Level A preceding it.

However, the andon is more than just an operational tool to manage flow, cost, and kanbans; it's a tool to promote mutual trust and respect within the community and the families of employees. In an advanced Lean system, the andon tells team members exactly how many minutes (if any) they will run overtime each day because the demand per hour is built into the system. At the end of the day, there is never a shocking realization that the team is behind. Each hour is visible, and the process and team members can get back on schedule by being more proactive, all based on takt time linked to the annual plan. The process is capable when man, material, method, and machine are planned for systematically.

### Developing Leaders in the Pilot Hall

The pilot hall needs a team leader who is chosen based on the long-term strategy and the organization's structure. Instead of hiring a team leader or developing a team leader from somewhere else in the organization, team members who embrace and live the culture daily in the pilot hall are chosen as the team leaders for the current or next pilot hall, depending on the current state of organizational structure. This helps perpetuate the culture and allows those who embrace the system and embody mutual trust and respect to permeate the organization. Through the pilot, these people can learn the tools and understand their connections within a frontline team. This begins to build a flexible, multifunctional workforce and also spreads the system. Using TPS long-term is the easiest way to change the culture, get results, and develop people from team members to CEO-level employees.

Leaders must use the pilot hall and teamwork strategy to hire and promote people who look and act like the system. It's a huge mistake to ignore this, especially as the system is maturing, because other people won't trust leadership or the system if individuals are promoted or hired who don't embody mutual trust/respect or fit the criteria or matrix. On the same note, those who don't fit the pilot culturally can do a lot of damage in a short period of time.

As mentioned earlier, it's the system that must hire and fire people, not individuals. Nonetheless, most companies hire people thinking, "Oh, she studied psychology at Harvard and has a 4.0 GPA; we need her in HR." However, if these individuals won't adopt cultural behaviors and aren't coachable, they will negatively affect the culture of the pilot and the organization. It's better to hire someone with a 2.5 GPA, cultural common sense, and an understanding of teamwork. The sensei, leaders, and even the system itself can teach a coachable person how to be smart in the system, be a team player, solve problems, and improve standard work. Thus, the most important element during an interview is determining whether a prospective employee fits within the culture.

Rodger's organizations eventually stopped looking at just colleges, degrees, and grades and started addressing culture and teamwork. All new hires went through a simulation, and if they didn't mimic the behaviors of the system during the simulation, they weren't hired. The whole system, including the human resources system, employee survey, the enablers, the hiring, and the training, matched, and people were selected into the pilot and the organization using the established matrix.

Human Resources is trained in using this Stars Matrix as well as in utilizing the master plan, sponsor the suggestion, and perfect attendance systems using the tools of Levels A and B. HR also must be able to put the roles and responsibilities into the performance appraisal system along with management cycle criteria, starting with executives.

All told, the criteria for entering the pilot become much more than simply entering that specific group; they become the criteria for entering the organization and integrating everyone else in it.

## EXECUTIVE'S ROLE IN THE PILOT HALL

The executive's role in the pilot hall is to do, learn, and go and see. The executive learns what the system operating at world class looks like and how to apply the tools to change processes and engage people. Executives work in the pilot hall as team members on the line a certain number of days per month in order to learn the role of other team members and how they apply to the role of an executive. Understanding those two functions helps executives understand how to move between implementation and support so they more deeply grasp how to coach and lead on a daily basis.

Executives must understand how to lead from the middle by doing the work, supporting the people, and coaching improvement. They don't learn a tool by reading books, going to conferences, or talking to experts—they actually employ total preventative maintenance, pull the andon, follow standard work, participate in daily meetings, start problem-solving sheets, do the 5 Whys, and make improvements. Executives can't and won't fully grasp how to coach until they work on the line and understand the process and people.

## Continuous Improvement Team in the Pilot Hall

The sensei needs to help the leader of the system, whether it's the leader of the CIP team, the executive leader, or an external coach, be responsible for helping the organization while holding a position of knowledge and skill. The organization must see that person, not the sensei, as the leader and star. It's never about the sensei; it's about building internal capability, beginning with trusting the leader.

The CIP team needs to be one step ahead of everybody else, including the pilot. If kanbans, team problem solving, team suggestions, etc., are going to be introduced, this team must first understand them from a theoretical standpoint in order to teach them in the pilot. Then the team will coach the tools and link them to the rest of the system as well as decide if others can coach or use them. Once the culture is established, the focus turns toward aligning the tools with the culture.

As the pilot matures and other departments/leaders advance into Level A, the organization may be ready for maturity audit one—a standardized cultural check of the Transformation Curve's tools—to ensure the continuous improvement team sees the same way and that leaders exhibit the behaviors that align with the system.

# CHAPTER 5

# Expanding Phase One with an Organizational Strategy

Generally, in the first year, executives look at the pilot hall and think, "Oh, it looks good…I understand the system. Let's spread this everywhere now." Usually this isn't possible, because expanding the system requires a plan.

In subsequent years, executives should have their own balanced scorecards as they learn how to lead as CEOs in the top down portion and pilots in their areas to support from the bottom up. The initial pilot thus goes deeper into the curve and develops other internal leaders to lead future pilots, using the first pilot hall to establish new pilot halls.

An organization can't simply dive into Phase One with one pilot area and then jump around to different areas based on need or want. There must be a long-term strategic plan to not only develop people and pilots but to link the entire organizational structure to the plan.

When the sensei and leader(s) define what the organization will look like in five or six years, they aren't merely addressing metrics and behaviors; they are also addressing what the organizational structure will look like.

Elements of organizational strategy of necessity include structure and compensation. (An infrastructure strategy must be developed simultaneously to align man, machine, material, and method.) This strategy must be developed from the onset of the Journey to World Class and, as mentioned earlier, must encompass a social pact that establishes mutual trust and respect. The sensei/leader must grasp how to achieve and fulfill the responsibilities of this social pact prior to committing to it and prior to fully embracing Level A of the Transformation Curve.

## A Closer Look at the Social Pact

Many organizations that understand an aim of the Toyota Production System (TPS) is to keep jobs and not lay off team members create social pacts between the organization and employees. Some who don't completely understand the foundations of a social pact make promises that no layoffs will occur from the elimination of waste. There must be a long-term strategic plan to support such a pact, or when the organization hits hard times, it won't be able to live up to its end of the bargain.

While creating a social pact is a critical part of developing mutual trust and respect, it must be aligned with the strategy, and the leader and sensei are responsible for making this possible. To start, the leader and sensei and generally HR need to link the pact to the strategy, grasping its headcount, products, services, and portfolio. For example, if an organization has 25,000 people and the sensei sees that there is 70% waste in that organization, s/he knows s/he could get rid of 70% of people. With 30% value added steps in the process, only 7,500 people would be necessary to run the business, if everything were running at 100%.

But is that really logical or even possible? Why would a sensei or leader want to do that? Looking at it the Toyota way, why not use the waste in the system to create an organizational structure that can sustain TPS and be world class?

Instead of eliminating waste to save money and decrease headcount, waste can be eliminated to create an organizational structure to maintain gains, eliminate more waste, and take on more products/services. The sensei must understand the balanced approach to drive out waste and establish an organizational structure for the long term. The social pact aspect of the plan helps establish a system that maintains mutual trust and respect even when unforeseeable hard times hit the organization.

Without a clear understanding of the strategy, the waste in the business portfolio, the ideal organizational strategy, and the Transformation Curve to eliminate waste, making a social pact is actually a false promise that the sensei and leader may be unable to fulfill. Should that happen, mutual trust and respect are violated and the culture is destroyed.

Likewise, a sensei cannot go into an organization and simply begin waving the social pact flag, promising that layoffs will never occur and the like. This would scare many executives, and the long-term plan would overwhelm them. They would doubt their ability to achieve the organizational strategy, and TPS might not take hold. The sensei must understand the business and the curve well enough to make a plan.

## Planning for Team Structure

In reality, only a small percentage of people will leave the organization. With this elimination of waste, many individuals can be moved to a team leader role to support the process, maintain the system, and make further improvements.

The target team structure is a ratio of one team leader to five team members in direct departments and 1:7 or 1:8 in indirect/support departments. Therefore, to put a TPS organizational structure in place—the plan—the headcount must be calculated based on team leaders, supervisors, etc., to get to this 1:5 ratio.

Once that plan is complete, it's necessary to look at temporary employees and relate this number back to the strategy to understand how much waste needs to be eliminated. When the sensei grasps what the head count number should be in five years, s/he and the leader are ready to make the social pact.

Using the Transformation Curve, a small percentage of the workforce should be contractional, depending on who is retiring when. If something goes wrong or the economy crashes and no one is buying the product or wants a service, the organization can keep its commitment to the social pact.

An organization should never lay off permanent employees, but contract team members may be let go as a last resort. The buffer depends on how solidified the business strategy is and the predicted attrition. If every year there is 5% turnover and contracted employees are 15% of the workforce, headcount can be reduced by 5% without affecting anyone and can be reduced by 20% without laying off any full-time employees.

When starting the Transformation Curve, senseis must grasp the current headcount, understand the business, and realize how much waste is in the organization and the processes. Knowing the target team ratio is 1:5 and that head count isn't going to change, senseis must grasp how much waste must be eliminated and how much they need to grow the business by to maintain the headcount and place team leaders throughout the organization. Roles and responsibilities must shift, and people must be prepared to be multifunctional.

Thus, when establishing a social pact, senseis must be forward thinking enough to also agree that employees will be multifunctional. In other words, just because individuals have certain jobs today doesn't necessarily mean they will be doing those same exact jobs in the future.

## Creating a Multifunctional Organization

No organization makes money paying the bills—it makes money making products, taking care of patients, or providing a value-added service to the customer. If a snowstorm prevents people from coming to work, everybody else has to fill in to keep the line running. This means the workforce must be multifunctional. A team structure of 1:5 linked throughout the organization to establish enough overlap on teams and within leadership helps people become multifunctional with a good plan linked to the balanced scorecard.

It is critical to establish Levels A and B before establishing the team structure, because if teams don't understand problem solving individually, how can they support team problem solving? If individuals aren't engaged in the suggestion system and making simple improvements, how can they be expected to make larger scale improvements within a team as problems arise? If the scorecard isn't established with check cycles and top problems visualized, how will the team be organized and know where to focus? The team structure helps advance the system, exposes more problems, and solves those problems linked to the balanced scorecard.

### True North for Being Multifunctional

At Toyota, everything from engineering to marketing to human resources to performance to recognition is all tied together and balanced. This means that organizational structure is vitally important. If it isn't defined and based upon leaders answering questions such as "Do I understand it? Can I do it? Can I coach it? Can I see it?", organizational structure is very difficult to manage.

If leaders cannot manage these questions and develop one-on-one relationships with those who report to them, the span of control is flawed. Thus, the leader is not a good leader and/or will not develop into a good leader due to the organizational structure.

When leaders really understand TPS, they understand their subordinates' jobs. This is because these leaders have worked all the jobs and can perform all these jobs. This is vital if they are to coach team members, but how many executives can do that?

When starting the Transformation Curve, the answer is, not many. However, after years spent learning the system, advancing in the curve, and promoting executives based on the Stars Matrix, the entire executive team should be multifunctional.

## Based on Skill, Not Time

If given the time, tools, and support necessary to become multifunctional, employees will work in that direction and will stand out, be promoted to team leaders, team leaders to supervisors, and so on until eventually the organization is where it planned to be. This can't happen overnight, though, and it must be linked to the five-year plan and beyond. Becoming a multifunctional organization takes time, but it's based on skill, not time. Maintaining the system along with implementing system audits will help keep the organization multifunctional and continually learning, but it starts with a plan linked to a compensation structure to reward people for being multifunctional, once Levels A and B are in place.

## Organizational Structure

If the organizational structure is too large for leaders to see problems, see opportunities, and coach, they won't even be able to hand out candy for suggestions. When that's the case, the Plan-Do-Check-Act (PDCA) cycle needs to be shortened by making sure the organizational structure is very flat, very lean, and very focused on maintaining the system.

More specifically, leaders can't wait until the end of the month to find out whether they are going to make their monthly targets. They need to find out by the hour. The whole goal is to ensure that if a problem occurs at the front line, there aren't 50 layers between the team member and the top leader to address the problem. If the organization is too complex, it can't get the right people involved at the right time and place to solve the problem or support the countermeasure. This means problems won't be solved or will be solved very slowly.

In one large global organization, a few major incidents occurred in a single year. The leader of the company sent out a group to investigate each one. Afterwards, he asked his sensei, "What should I have done? How should I have responded?"

Rodger told the leader he should have gone to investigate, get the facts, and support problem solving. However, because his span and responsibility were so vast, the president couldn't even get out of his office.

As far as the PDCA cycle was concerned, this leader was so far away from the point of cause that he couldn't impact the countermeasure to address the problem. From a behavior standpoint, he had no ownership of the problem or countermeasure. Behaviorally, all he was doing was demanding a problem-solving countermeasure that didn't promote or support mutual trust and respect. Command and control with no bottom up support does not align with the cultural expectations of the Toyota Production System.

The leader must be able to perform PDCA on the master plans, the balanced scorecards, the process, and the people, but how can a leader check master plans if there are 60 of them? How can a leader do the PCDA cycle daily?

Span of control is very important both logistically and systematically. The leader has to be able to touch the team on a frequent basis to see the positive and support the balanced scorecard. If the organization is too matrixed or too large, the leader and TPS will fail. This means the organizational structure, the systematic plan, and the maturity audits must all fit together. If they are not tied into an overall system and culture, they cannot be successful.

That's why the check (maturity audit one) in Phase One is a cultural check. The focus is on trying to move the culture and teach the behaviors. As the organization is streamlined to the organizational strategy—the plan—the sensei and leader need to be more focused on the cultural aspects of adapting TPS. Executives need to shift from being strategic leaders to "go-and-seers," and their checks have to occur at least daily and eventually hourly. This means the organizational structure must be streamlined so that the executives are closer to the point of cause, helping solve problems as they occur, proactively.

Becoming a multifunctional organization and multifunctional in the pilot is vitally important. Rather than having five people standing around, there might be two, and if they're multifunctional, an andon will immediately pull the person who needs to come. For the process to be capable, the engineering or quality or logistics team member doesn't need to stand there and watch. These individuals respond where they are needed within the allowable timeframe, but it starts with creating teamwork, establishing the team structure within the pilot, and maintaining the process using proactive andons.

## Organizational Compensation

Compensation for the mass of the organization is made up of base compensation, qualification compensation, involvement in the Continuous Improvement Program, and organizational performance. Team members will get their base wages but will also have the opportunity to achieve higher pay through suggestions, team leader certification/qualification, perfect attendance, and achieving the balanced scorecard as a department and organizationally. An example payment structure is seen in Figure 5.1 below.

| | | |
|---|---|---|
| A | Base | $15 |
| B | Multi-Functional | $1 |
| C | TL Qualification | $1 |
| D | Suggestions | $2 |
| E | Perfect Attendance | $2 |
| F | Profit Sharing | $2 |
| | Total Potential | $23 |

**Figure 5.1**

Executive compensation is based on salary and achieving targeted performance goals as visualized on the balanced scorecard. This is introduced and elaborated on in the management cycle but is not covered in this book.

## Suggestion System Rewards

Rewarding suggestions monetarily is a voluntary way for team members to make more money over and above their base wages by having the most creative/innovative suggestions. Team members could potentially submit 20 suggestions and receive $1,000. If one of the suggestions is chosen as the most creative and innovative, this individual could receive $50 as a monthly winner, $100 as a quarterly winner, and $1,000 as a yearly winner, depending on the policy. Under this system, each team member has the opportunity to make $2,500 dollars extra every year or even more. A team member can make the base pay, base pay + $1000, or base pay + $2500+. All the leader has to do is make suggestions available and teach people how to use them, then go, see, encourage, and recognize the reward. This is a very simple yet very powerful way to change the culture and achieve world-class results.

## Multifunctional Compensation

The compensation structure supports the desired team structure—pay is linked to the workforce being multifunctional. This way, when a team leader is ready to be a supervisor, another qualified team member can immediately step in to be the team leader. The system is built on mutual trust and respect and hires and fires people, so not only does everyone know who is the most qualified based on the matrix and structure, but the team member already knows what his or her additional compensation is going to be when entering the team leader role. Promotions aren't based on concepts such as "You look like me"; they are based on the system.

Base pay is the same for team members and team leaders. Thus, team members might make $10 per hour as a base but also have additional ways to make more money. They can implement individual and team suggestions, take training to become team leader qualified, and support the teams above and below them to get a bonus linked to the balanced scorecard. The only way a team member can make more money on an hourly basis is to either be qualified multifunctional or to support the system and help the team/organization achieve balanced scorecard targets. Executives are not paid for suggestions but must also be multifunctional.

## Organization-Wide Profit Sharing

The financial success of team members and employees should be based on the success of the organization achieving world-class status as defined by the balanced scorecard. Striving to perpetuate mutual trust and respect and eliminating waste will create more success. The system is not about lining the pockets of owners, shareholders, executives, etc. without employees taking part in that success. Organization-wide profit sharing is a way to link balanced scorecard results to everyone's compensation and the organization's success to achieve more results down the road.

Like any other component of the system, profit sharing must be paid for by the elimination of waste—leaders can't expect customers to pay for it. If the organization, including the owners, shareholders, and community, generally has a 5% profit margin, an agreement or policy can be established for how excess money will be divided.

### *Prorated by Priority*

The whole system is based on improvement and achieving the balanced scorecard metrics—that is how everyone achieves a bonus. Furthermore, it's prorated, meaning that compensation is higher for safety and quality than it is for finance in order to reinforce the priorities, similar to how the suggestion system points are established. The bonus for safety, quality, productivity, human development, and cost may be 35%, 25%, 20%, 15%, and 10%, respectively. This reinforces safety as the number one priority, further promotes mutual trust and respect by demonstrating that the system is not about cost, and provides a clear way for all employees to know exactly what results need to be realized in order to achieve a bonus.

### *Team Profit Sharing, Not Individual*

The actual results on the balanced scorecard are the only way employees, from the CEO to the frontline team member, can get bonuses. In other words, bonuses are linked to results and are stacked—supervisors don't get bonuses unless their direct reports get bonuses. The CEO doesn't get a bonus unless everyone else gets one. A CEO's bonus is based on all the people who directly report to him or her. Furthermore, bonuses for executives, supervisors, and other leaders are tied to what their direct reports get and also what their peers get. If everyone on the team is a supervisor and one person is eligible for 4%, one is at 2%, and two others are at 6%, then everyone might only get 2%. Leaders must help other leaders achieve balanced scorecard results so that if they don't work as a team supporting each other, it's going to carry over to everyone's bonus (or lack thereof) at the end of the year.

Based on the teamwork model, if the team isn't helping each other, their peers, the teams above, and the teams below, they all get the same scores tied to the profit sharing. For example, if a subordinate comes to his or her leader and asks, "Why am I only getting a 3% bonus when I should be getting 6%?" the leader can say, "Well, you know Joe and all your other team members you were to work with…Did you help them get a 6%?"

It's about teamwork—not just soft teamwork but teamwork linked to results and linked to personal compensation. Individuals must support their teams, the teams above, below, and side to side, and it all relates back to compensation and the maturity audits. It's about paying for performance—team performance within the overall organizational strategy.

Additional strategies can stabilize and extend implementation, but the organizational strategy, because of its link to compensation, team structure, and the social pact, must be grasped from the onset of the Transformation Curve.

# Chapter 6

# Sustaining Continuous Improvement through Audits

Maturity audits check the status of transformation against the standard, based on the phase of implementation. The audit has three parts, introduced after each of the three phases.

The first audit, introduced after the cultural change phase, is the cultural portion of the maturity audit. The second maturity audit checks how well the organization is implementing and adapting the Toyota Production System (TPS). The third audit focuses on daily living and maintaining the system.

These audits can be simple and behaviorally driven or very complex and results driven.

## Maturity Audit One

The tools of this book only utilize maturity audit one, introduced after the cultural change phase, but an understanding of maturity audits two and three helps paint a picture of where the organization is moving on its Journey to World Class. Grasping how to link the organizational strategy with maturity audits two and three will help executives engage in an organizational strategy and a social pact.

## Check the Culture First

Organizations that focus on just achieving results and using tools haven't been able to sustain adaptations of TPS. This is typically due to a neglect of culture and behaviors while overemphasizing results. These organizations do not achieve sustained success because they haven't put the culture in place that endures through generations of leadership, team members, and the organization. Therefore, the sensei and leader need to look for behaviors and try to improve the culture.

Maturity audit one is very simple; it checks to see how teams are tracking against the standards as seen in behaviors and artifacts. Is there a balanced scorecard? Is it visual? Is there a daily meeting focused on balanced scorecard priorities? Is there a proactive fourth row? Is the team problem solving according to the standard? Is there follow-up of problem solving? Is there a plan linked to the balanced scorecard? Is the plan visualized and checked?

This audit checks the simple tools and the visuals and behaviors within the artifacts. The results are segmented using symbols—an X, a triangle, and a triangle inside a circle. The symbols essentially mean "does not exist," "needs improvement," and "the improvement is controlled," respectively. Symbols are used instead of numbers to keep the conversation focused on an approximation of the status versus exact numbers. The results are usually shown via a radar chart or spider diagram listing the tools and how the team is progressing along the above three options.

## Learning to See the Same

In terms of the Continuous Improvement Program, the purpose of audit one is to get everyone on the same page. There isn't necessarily a right or wrong answer to the status of a tool or behavior, but all members of the continuous improvement team and leadership should be consistent in their observation and communication of the status. They must come to the same conclusion and agree on the system.

As with the other tools, the audit starts in the pilot hall. If the continuous improvement team and leaders can't agree on what they see, how can they coach and/or communicate the standard consistently throughout the organization? Therefore, all members of the continuous improvement team must go to the pilot and use the audit to generate results. They must check to see if the results are consistent and identify inconsistencies among the team to gain consensus.

Once the results are the same, their ability to see is the same. Now the audit can be published. It's not opinionated, and the discussion is focused on the necessary improvements. This is another example of the system being based on mutual trust and respect and creating a new level of learning for the organization.

The continuous improvement team must learn to see the same before advancing the system to other pilots. If these team members aren't consistent, it will be a nightmare for the executive leaders and the sensei. They will let the system spread throughout the organization without focusing on the pilot and maintaining consistency. It will be very difficult for the organization to learn, and transformation won't occur, or at the very least will take a long time.

Members of the continuous improvement team need to progress at the same rate and come to the same conclusions before coaching other areas. If one of the pilots isn't progressing at the same rate, the sensei and leader must help problem solve, because they are ultimately responsible. If the continuous improvement team doesn't agree on the standards of audit one—if individuals coach and audit to different standards—it's the sensei's fault. That's why all continuous improvement team members must agree to the standards in the pilot and be coached and monitored by the sensei. This team must see consistently so that people trust the audit and mutual respect is preserved.

## Scoring Audit One

In later audits, scoring is essential. However, audit one uses symbols to visualize status because at this point, it's impossible to measure the gap between the current and the standard using a precise measurement. In other words, putting numbers to the audit is confusing and focuses attention on the number rather than the improvement needed to advance the culture and system.

In this phase, the goal is for everyone who is auditing/being audited to interpret the standard and the exception the same. Then, the conversation can focus on improvement rather than the actual score, which advances mutual trust and respect. If everyone agrees on the standard, nobody will point out differences in the score. This way, the auditor isn't attacked. People will understand the results and make improvements. Once a team is at this level, trusting the auditors, trusting the audit, and trusting the system, they can begin auditing themselves.

## Self-Auditing

Self-auditing can occur once everyone sees consistently. Teams shouldn't audit themselves until self-auditing works in the pilot. The pilot shouldn't audit itself until the continuous improvement team can audit and agree on the standard. Once this team has the same understanding of the audit, they coach other teams to audit and integrate the audit into the rest of the system.

Everyone must aim for the same standard, regardless of whether they are an executive, team leader, supervisor, or continuous improvement team member. The sensei and the continuous improvement team can see, and now the pilot leaders can see. Once everybody gets to the same level of being able to see and this is reflected in the culture, one person can say, "It's a triangle." People won't argue with the results; they will focus on the improvement, and the seeing will happen much more frequently than just during an audit.

## Once Again, the Emphasis Is on Skill, Not Time

Some leaders will say, "Oh, I can do it fast. I can implement this system faster than anyone here." Remember, the standard audit is to check and look for behaviors. Only when the behaviors and tools are in place per the standard can the team move to the next level. Leaders can go as fast as they want, but until the skill is developed, they shouldn't move to the next tool. As discussed previously, the system is based on skill, not time. Maturity audits are based on facts, behaviors, and results, not on where someone thinks he or she is. These audits focus on achievement using the balanced scorecard, the checks, visual management, and so on.

## Maturity Audit Two

The second audit, maturity audit two, is typically introduced after Phase Two, after people's hearts and minds are captured. This audit checks that people are relating their hearts and minds to achieving results. For example, it's not enough to have a daily meeting and do problem solving. The problem solving must be proactive; it must impact results proactively rather than reactively. Kanban systems must not only be in place but must also be linked to results, cash flow, inventory turns, and finance metrics. Andons must be in place, not as a command and control call for help but as a strategic and frequent call for help linked to one-piece flow and proactive problem solving linked to the balanced scorecard.

Maturity audit two checks that behaviors drive results proactively.

## Shifting from Reactive to Proactive

In maturity audit two, leaders move from reactive to proactive. This means that certain expectations are achieved linking behaviors to results. Audit two checks whether teams are moving from reactive key performance indicators to proactive key performance indicators, if master plans drive results proactively, or if teams wait for problems to occur, solving them reactively. It also checks whether leaders spread the suggestions that impact results throughout the organization.

Maturity audit two is much more detailed than maturity audit one, and results are expected as well as behaviors and cultural artifacts. In addition, all those expectations are linked with the balanced scorecard, the leaders' evaluation, and to the overall outcome at the end of the year. Payments, bonuses, and overall compensation are linked to the balanced scorecard, making it very clear to leaders and peers who exhibits the behaviors and links the results.

Maturity audit two is transparent; it uses the established PCDA cycles (daily meetings, monthly meetings, proactive checks) and the sixth column of the balanced scorecard. The audit must be visualized on the leadership level, with everyone knowing the score and which leaders are behind. Leaders' two options are to achieve the audit score proactively or reactively.

Achieving the score proactively ensures that the balanced scorecard and master plan are linked very tightly and that master plans drive daily actions and behaviors. Achieving the score reactively means that the leader and sensei have performed an audit and determined that the standard is not in place, and the leader with the low score performs kaizen to get back on track. This helps both advance and sustain the system.

To proactively impact audit two means making a good annual plan with a mix of kaizen events, quality circles, team suggestions, and individual suggestions. Leaders need to ensure that all people are trained, that they are multifunctional at work, and that they follow and improve the process. Managing activities proactively ensures that leaders will get a good score as well as achieve the results expected in later maturity audits. If leaders aren't doing this proactively, they will do it reactively. It's the sensei's job to help top leaders increase the frequency of audits so that leaders managing reactively will begin to manage proactively or exit the organization.

### Scoring Audit Two

Using maturity audit two, the check becomes more defined and the standards clearer. There is less arguing about the audit and its results because people can see what the standard is, see the balanced scorecard results, and see that there is a discrepancy. People begin to focus on the point of occurrence and the actual problem more than the audit results. At this point, there can be an actual score to the audit ranging from 0 to 5. Generally, people won't argue with the score because they trust the process and the people. They understand focusing on the gray zone to make improvements, and they know it's not a punitive tool.

In Phase Three, the audit is used as an organizational development and flexibility tool, and the score is necessary to provide a more sophisticated detail of the result than the symbols provided in audit one.

### Frequency of Auditing

Maturity audit one should be done regularly, for example monthly, as part of the balanced scorecard check cycle. When maturity audit one is working in Phases One and Two and is maintained into Phase Three, leaders might do it monthly or every two months. An executive and sensei might do the audit monthly in each department, linking team leader and group leader. If the leader chooses to react to a negative score (instead of being proactive), everyone gets a bad score. People will know which team members are keeping them from achieving a bonus because the score is very transparent and visual.

## Maturity Audit Three

The last audit, maturity audit three, is the world-class audit. It is very well defined, with artifacts such as an annual plan, proactive key performance indicators on the balanced scorecard, hourly or at least daily checks to ensure targets are met, and a number of other artifacts to continually sustain and improve people and processes. In this world-class scenario, checks are directed and strong because people's hearts and minds are engaged. The sequenced toolbox supports the team and organization moving from phase to phase, solving problems in an ever-decreasing gray zone.

In Phase Three, leaders don't wait until the end of the week, month, or quarter, which is generally reactive. In Phase Three, leaders perform the audits because they understand TPS deeply and have learned how the organization works on an intimate level. Leaders now understand how hourly/daily checks impact them and the balanced scorecard, along with their own and their team's compensation.

This is the essence of maintaining the system, and it also explains why maintaining is much more difficult than improving. Many organizations, leaders, and processes have been improved, yet very few maintain and sustain the improvements.

## Scoring Maturity Audit Three

In maturity audit two, people learn to trust the auditing process and the score. The conversation focuses on improving rather than the score itself. In maturity audit three, the score is very specific and important because it becomes a true measurement tool. If an individual or team isn't achieving balanced scorecard results, the problem's origination is very clear because the audit scores are published and transparent. In this phase, people don't argue with the audit anymore. They look at the standard and the results and see the discrepancy. This phase is more defined because the grey zone is smaller and not everybody can see it.

The first audit is about being a circle triangle (meeting expectations). If a person is above expectations, that's great, but it's not designed for people to be above expectations. In Phase Two, a score is associated with the audit and is published, but people may still be uncertain about the meaning of the score.

In Phase Three and beyond, especially when the audit is being published and used as an improvement tool, many leaders will misrepresent the score. They will self-report a much higher score than what they actually have. Typically, departments that claim to be a 4.5 or 5 do not score that high. If they actually score a 4.5 or 5, it means they are stagnant and not improving. If they are a 4.5 or a 5 consistently, they aren't moving around the good people, creating skills within the organization, and likewise aren't multifunctional enough.

## Frequency of Auditing

With maturity audit three, the leader and sensei force a person, team, or organization to be proactive, as the audit is performed randomly. It may be performed on a frequent basis and linked visually to the balanced scorecard, but the leader and sensei use random audits to validate existing results and to see what in the system is broken and what results might have been missed. If leaders don't achieve their required score on a random audit, they will be responsible for performing a kaizen event to get back on target with the audit and results. This keeps most leaders in a proactive mode, as they realize that being proactive is better for themselves and their teams.

Using the management cycle and the foundations introduced in Level A—Plan-Do-Check-Act, visual management, and roles and responsibilities—the sensei audits those who aren't achieving their goals on the balanced scorecard. Again, this isn't punitive but rather helps the individual and the team succeed. The leader and sensei must remain proactive and help other leaders be proactive. Audits are linked to the business case if there is an actual or potential problem that will or might lead to missed targets. In Phase Three, audits are based on the leader's and sensei's judgment regarding potential problems with insufficient proactive measures in place.

## A Note on Compensation

The audit is a necessary supplement to the balanced scorecard and the master plan, as its aim is to see where fine improvements are needed. The third audit is more stringent and focused because it's much more difficult to identify the improvements needed. Everyone must trust the audit and realize it's an improvement tool to help achieve balanced scorecard targets, not a control or punishment tool linked to compensation.

Audits help achieve results, so the bonus system and audit are not linked. No one gets a bonus because of a good audit score; likewise, no one is penalized for a poor audit score. The bonus system is linked to the balanced scorecard—the performance of the team and organization—and the audit is an improvement tool to help achieve the balanced scorecard. Once the culture is in place and people understand the audit results are for improvement and not for control, they won't try to misrepresent or overstate the results. They will want a more specific audit to help them see a smaller gray zone so they can achieve their balanced scorecard targets.

## Sustaining a Multifunctional Workforce

The further into the curve an organization moves, the more multifunctional people become. The organizational strategy compensates people based on skill, not time. Promotions and raises are based on skill and being multifunctional. People spend more time on cross-functional problem-solving teams. Leaders perform audits to learn how to see in other departments, help coach, and soon have a chance to lead different departments.

It is very difficult for an organization to score a 4 on maturity audit three. If becoming and sustaining a world-class organization is the goal, being multifunctional is necessary. Therefore, within TPS, every time a leader or supervisor achieves a score of a 3.5 (for example), the sensei or executive leader forces the organization, the department, or the leader from a 3.5 to a 2.75 so that the person, team, or organization is challenged to improve. This is done by rotating and changing people's positions, bringing on a new product or service line, or doing something else to cause a disturbance and generate more improvement. The goal is not to be a 5; the goal is to be an improving organization with a multifunctional workforce aimed at being world class.

At Toyota, for example, a manager from one area that's doing great may be told, "Okay, Joe, it's been three years; you're going to run the body shop now."

Joe may never have run a body shop before, but a world class organization doesn't necessarily care about previous direct experience leading a certain process or department. A team leader, manager, supervisor, etc. doesn't need to "know how to run a body shop," because s/he understands TPS, embodies the culture, and knows how the tools overlap, so s/he can learn to run any part of the organization very quickly.

Of course, the maturity audit score will drop down a bit, but it will eventually come back up. This process checks to ensure that the leader/department doesn't drop down too far, impacting results that will impact the customer. It's also a way to know, by the score, when it's time to rotate leaders in order to sustain a multifunctional organization.

## Beyond Maturity Audit Three

Beyond Phase Three, it isn't necessary to complete any of the audits frequently. They are used proactively. The real check is an external check. For this, Toyota uses J.D. Power and Associates. Other organizations may use different but similar world-class checks.

Every year, Toyota Georgetown had a J.D. Power and Associates check. In January, Rodger would write the score down on a piece of paper and put it in an envelope and give it to his team members. He always accurately predicted the J.D. Power and Associates score, and people always wondered how. One day, Rodger answered their question.

"Remember the checks we do every day? It's in my master plan. We know what to check, we know the targets, and we know how we match up against the targets."

If the system is right, the check will equal the desired intent, but checks must start with cultural change so that the people trust the check and use it for improvement rather than control.

# Chapter 7

# Phase Two, Level C

In Phase Two, Level C, the team/organization is culturally prepared for operational improvements, more so than previously. By now, certain basics have been established, such as a Continuous Improvement Program (CIP) with individual suggestions, team suggestions, and kaizen events. Executives are engaged in seeing the positive and recognizing positive behaviors at the front line. The management cycle is established and ingrained in performance evaluations and standard work. An organizational strategy exists to sustain the gains and support proactive problem solving, and the culture reflects mutual trust and respect. The entire organization—a team of teams—is pointed in the right direction toward becoming world class, and the elimination of waste is a mindset, not the elimination of jobs.

## Tools of Phase Two, Level C

Phase Two, Level C introduces new tools such as one-page reports, one-piece flow, perfect attendance, meeting facilitation, effective listening, and the five-minute rule. Phase Two, Level C is shown in Figure 7.1 on the next page. Many of the tools introduced in this phase are well-known Lean tools that are typically only presented in a mature Lean system. Some people try to use these tools without grasping Levels A and B, thinking they can implement them successfully without the culture in place, but cultural change must come before implementation if these tools are to be useful and sustainable.

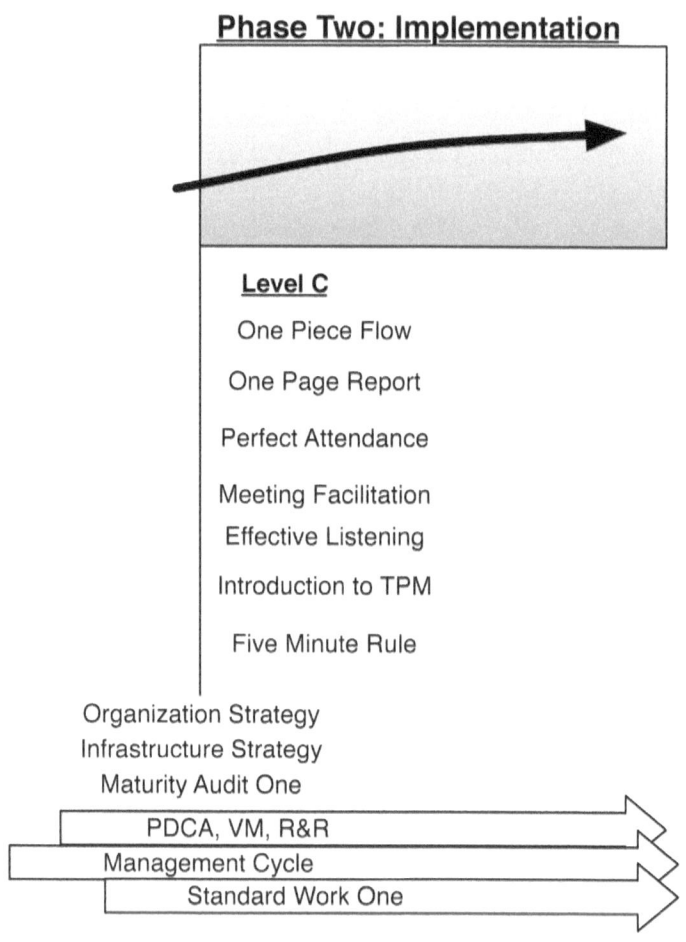

Figure 7.1

## Cultural Change before Implementation

To recap, most Lean leaders and thinkers don't understand the importance of cultural change before changing the work. Forcing people do to things and then drawing them in to make improvements doesn't work and isn't sustainable. People need to understand, be engaged and enabled, and know why they're doing what they're doing before they begin to improve standard work.

Standard work must be sequenced at the right time within the curve. Yes, the work must be changed, but why would anyone want to go into an organization screaming that the work must be changed? Hearing "We have to change the work!" and being thrown on a kaizen event team to redesign the work doesn't necessarily engage anyone. Why not start with changing behaviors, recognizing the positive, and leading people into changing the work?

It's possible to go into a company without Phase One in place and total preventative maintenance of the system and tell employees, "You either follow the standard or you won't work here," but are employees going to trust and respect the sensei or leader or organization, or will they simply do what they're told because they have to, until they can find a new job?

If an organization is culturally oriented and focused on positive behavior, it won't want employees to follow the new system just because they have to; it will want them to change and standardize the work because they want to, because it's linked to the balanced scorecard, and because there is reinforcement recognizing the positive.

## Standard Work One, a Phase Two Foundation

The foundations of Level C are Plan-Do-Check-Act (PDCA), visual management, roles and responsibilities, and the management cycle. In Level C, or when transitioning into Level C, the foundation called standard work one is introduced to link the systems to the process and to outcomes.

At first, Toyota's concept of standard work must be simplified to mesh with cultural change, aimed towards world class. Toyota's version of standard work is far too complex for many organizations, even world-class organizations. To think that anyone can start out with true standard work is a mistake. The goal of the basic introduction of standard work one is to make the outcome consistent, using work instruction sheets, work description sheets, or other tools before attempting standard work two and full-blown standard work like Toyota's.

This way, people are able to grasp how the outcome of simple standard work is related to the balanced scorecard and how standard work one effects the outcome. It's an obvious next step to begin using standardization to get reliable outcomes. The most important element to standard work one is creating repeatability in the process in terms of safety, quality, productivity, and cost.

## Standard Work at Toyota

At Toyota, the goal of standard work is to identify safety, quality, and productivity issues, to see non-value added, and to obtain reliability. Standardized work at Toyota is very detailed—it's about standard sequence, standard timing, and line balancing, and it relies on the andon system. It's all linked and very, very complex.

The system is based on takt time and aligns with the one-piece-flow strategy. At Toyota, if a car is produced every 60 seconds, the rest of the system is based on 60 seconds. That means that any team that's involved with the moving line that produces a car is equalized around 90%. Thus, every minute that everyone is working an average around 90% leaves six seconds (10% of 60 seconds) for non-motion. Thus, six seconds of that minute is motion oriented in order to identify value, non-value to eliminate, and non-value added work.

Again, the theory is that if a team has five people and the work can actually be done with four, the fifth person isn't eliminated. That person, or the time that equals a person, is dedicated toward total preventative maintenance of the system and the process—to respond to andons, make improvements, participate in kaizen events, and become a team leader or supervisor qualified.

Again, this is very complex. Explaining it to an organization's executive wouldn't be useful, as they wouldn't be able to comprehend its ramifications, let alone implement Toyota's version of standard work. Standard work one introduces standard work strategically to an organization and is the foundation of more advanced versions of standard work.

## One-Piece Flow

The concept of one-piece flow linked to the foundation of standard work one creates an element of visibility in the process that is necessary to solve problems in the moment. In Level C, product flows one piece at time with no buffers, and supplies for that main product are with parts that match it. Eventually, everything will be flowing based on takt time, but initially, it must flow one piece at a time.

If the product isn't being pulled one piece at a time, andon can't be applied, because it's too late to take the problem to its source. With no buffer in the line, quality has to be 100% with no rejects. The outcome has to be the same every time. To achieve 100% quality at takt time right away usually isn't possible without impacting the customer, which is why the pilot hall is so important.

One-piece flow must be introduced to the pilot first so that buffers can be at the end of the line and the customer isn't impacted. The pilot hall must demonstrate the new standard for the rest of the organization—one-piece flow based on standard work one to achieve reliable outcomes.

If one-piece flow isn't introduced in the pilot hall, it will be very difficult for people to link it to the rest of the system. What's more, if the behaviors aren't in place—the go and sees, proactive problem solving, recognition of further waste elimination—one-piece flow won't work. Everyone must grasp the team member's role and that of the team leaders, supervisors, executives, and so on. They must begin to grasp value versus non-value added so that more waste can be eliminated.

*VALUE VERSUS NON-VALUE ADDED*

At Toyota (and other world-class organizations), many consultants, leaders, and organizations teach employees the difference between "value added" and "non-value added" as well as "The 8 Wastes." These are important concepts that must be taught to every employee, but at the right time.

Teaching about wastes and waste elimination when starting the Lean journey can have a negative outcome if people have no mechanism to elevate a problem, no way to make suggestions, and no opportunity for leaders to come and see the positive waste eliminated. Teaching about the different wastes too early can also imply that people make waste. It implies that wasted motion, overproduction, and transportation can all be eliminated. By extension, once they are eliminated, people can be eliminated, because the work has improved.

If people don't understand the organizational strategy of eliminating waste to create team leaders, engage in total preventative maintenance of the system, and make additional improvements, a social pact will not provide the mutual trust and respect that allows people to recognize and eliminate waste.

When the organization, starting with the pilot hall, is ready to learn standard work, using simple job instruction sheets that are followed by every person on every shift creates reliable outcomes. Leaders and executives must be ready to check to see that not only is the outcome reliable but that the process is followed, thus eliminating more waste. Andon one must be in place to respond to anything abnormal—not just the outcome but any anomalies in the process.

When people have clear work instructions and clear inputs/outputs, they can spot an abnormality immediately and pull the andon so that the right person can respond. The standard becomes clearer, which makes it easy for team members and team leaders to do the 5 Whys and bring the irregular outcome directly to its source while eliminating the root cause. Value added and non-value added are taught to spark more creative suggestions and to help employees learn to see.

## One-Page Reports

As the system matures, the go and sees are in place to reinforce positive improvements. At this point in the Transformation Curve, executives grasp and help solve top problems before monthly meetings, while team members solve problems on a daily basis through the suggestion system, individual problem solving, and team problem solving.

Though meetings are still necessary, they become more focused and succinct so leaders continue to go, see, and maintain the system. One leader will have more than just one pilot hall and may not have time for every full-blown monthly meeting. One-page reports, generally put on A3 size paper, communicate proposals, problems, status, or other information to support necessary meetings and face-to-face communication. These reports are a way to summarize charts, activities, problems, and the future plan so face-to-face communication is efficient.

### One-Page Status Reports

The one-page status report is a way to summarize the scoreboard charts and visualize the future plan, top problems, and critical actions, all on one piece of paper. Meetings can be wasteful, but they are necessary to start PDCA.

As PDCA cycles are refined, the one-page report is a great way to increase the efficiency of check cycles so that PDCA can be done daily, even hourly. Too much waste and too many ineffective meetings inhibit shorter PDCA and daily proactive problem solving. More importantly, meetings take time away from leaders to go and see and recognize the positive.

Whether the one-page report is used to support a monthly or weekly review, once it's standardized, it's easy to do. Generally, everyone involved in a new plan signs off on the one-page report prior to the leader meeting with the person or group receiving the one-page report. The leader can then quickly grasp and confirm the status of all his or her areas and create a summary of the one-page reports.

For example, if an inpatient director has multiple direct reports who manage multiple inpatient units, each leader creates a one-page report for his or her unit that can be summarized for a face-to-face discussion with his or her one-up. However, go and sees and visuals like the scorecard should be established or the PDCA cycle won't have a strong foundation. Remember, the goal is to have daily or hourly checks, and the one-page report should aim towards that goal but must be supported by the rest of the system.

Monthly meetings in Levels A and B are generally reactive to problems. Whereas in Level C, monthly meetings become more proactive and are linked to hoshin. In Level C, problems should be more focused, with leaders spending more time going and seeing. Summarizing the scoreboard, master plans, and so on in a one-page report gives leaders more time to go and see and to confirm what the one-page report says. PDCA becomes part of the culture because leaders realize that if the sensei, executive leader, or manager gets a one-page report from his or her area, that person lives and practices PDCA daily and will go see, check, and confirm the one-page report, learning how best to support improvement.

The system becomes very transparent because the one-page report summarizes the scorecards and master plans and the leader confirms them. Therefore, scoreboards must be in place prior to the one-page report so that leaders know before they see the report where targets are missed. It's difficult to "cover up" or to mislead a leader when scorecards are transparent, visual, and checked prior to the one-page report cycle.

Good executives using the one-page report in a mature system will know if a leader is not being truthful and transparent because they are already out on the floor reviewing scorecards; they already know if a missed target exists. In many cases, the leader already knows what the one-page report will say. The communication process simply validates that the leaders and executives are on the same page. If they are not on the same page, the executive knows whose master plan to focus on during master plan checkpoints, not as a punitive action but rather to support the rest of the team.

## Problem-Solving One-Page Reports

As the Continuous Improvement Program continues into kaizen events and quality circles, a one-page report may be necessary to summarize the findings of the kaizen activity—team problem solving, problem solving two, kaizen events, and quality circles. Some consultants take kaizen events and then add fancy presentation reports at the end to summarize events to a fault. Though it shows respect to have leaders hear the report, once events become part of the culture, respect is shown by going and seeing the new improvements and supporting the new process with checks.

The problem-solving one-page report helps leaders quickly get up to speed on what to go and see, what the remaining problems are, and the major process improvements from the event. Events and team problem solving must be integrated into the culture, and the one-page report becomes a standard report for leaders to communicate the status of a problem and improvement activity.

A problem-solving one-page report may include the analysis from problem solving two such as Pareto charts and Fishbone diagrams and may be linked to multiple problem-solving sheets with multiple root causes. As individual team members become more skilled in problem solving one, many problems can be solved using the suggestion system or problem-solving sheets. When problems rise to the level of a top problem that must involve teamwork, they tend to be more advanced problems that take a higher level of analysis, problem solving, and follow-up. The problem-solving one-page reports helps in that manner.

## Don't Rush to One-Page Reports

People must understand that problem solving one, problem solving two, individual suggestions, team suggestions, and so on must work before the one-page report can function as intended. If teams don't understand leading and lagging indicators, if the fourth row of the balanced scoreboard isn't working well to proactively identify process problems, if leaders aren't going to see, it's difficult to grasp how one-page reports support a team and how the leader can use them to validate, recognize, and coach.

Sure, one-page reports are a great tool to coach people. Some consultants teach that one-page reports or A3s are a great way to start Lean Transformation. However, if people can't do simple 5 Whys on a basic problem-solving sheet, how will they be able to do the 5 Whys in their heads? If they can't manage proactive measures in the fourth row of the scoreboard, how can they identify proactive opportunities on a daily basis? If teams don't have a willingness and eagerness to make change, how will leaders culturally implement and sustain the improvement that is documented on a one-page report?

If the culture isn't in place, the one-page report will become another tool for command and control, which may result in improvements but typically isn't sustainable and violates mutual trust and respect. The culture must be in place for the one-page report to be a standard that reinforces the positive and helps leaders better engage within the system.

Toyota uses one-page reports because the culture has been in place for years. Think problem solving, positive recognition, just-in-time, and other tools. Just-in-time isn't just about supplies and product; it's also about information—data, numbers, etc., all on a one-page report. This tool isn't in Levels A or B, because if people begin creating too many reports, they get afraid of negative consequences, since the culture isn't in place. This is the same reason maturity audit one isn't introduced until after Level B.

Introducing one-page reports (A3s) too early is a mistake, because leaders need the rest of the system in place both to confirm and support the information on the one-page report. If individuals can't put the information on a one-page report, their balanced scorecard is not visual enough, the PDCA cycle isn't working, and the system isn't mature enough to warrant it. If they can't take the balanced scorecard charts and summarize them on the top left quadrant of a one-page report along with the future plan, the leader either needs more focus or the one-page report has been introduced too early.

If, on the other hand, leaders are given a one-page report but don't grasp how to go and see and the importance of it, they will use command and control without bottom up support. The one-page report will then become another way for leaders to call and give orders, which is not the purpose of the tool.

## Perfect Attendance

In Level C, the concept of perfect attendance is introduced, which is another component of the Transformation Curve that helps organizations focus on the positive and reward those individuals who have perfect attendance.

## *Reinforcing the Positive*

The perfect attendance system reinforces the positive and supports the team structure. When the 1:5 ratio is in place, team leaders cover for team members who are on vacation or sick and can't come to work. Vacations are easy to plan, but sick days and call offs can disrupt the process and are more difficult to anticipate, which makes it more difficult to become a multifunctional workforce.

Team leaders can cover for team members when they are sick, but if it happens too often, or if too many team members call off at the same time, team leaders can't respond to andons or maintain the system.

The perfect attendance system helps reinforce the standard of coming to work, while the Continuous Improvement Program engages people so that they want to come to work. Ultimately, it's about mutual trust and respect and maintaining the system, linked to the balanced scorecard, and built into the compensation plan when targets are hit.

The perfect attendance system is just another way to recognize behaviors and get everybody to want to come to work. Leaders shouldn't talk about negative attendance. Instead, leaders who understand the system and have a plan will say, "We have a multifunctional organization, and this week we want to cross train five people. However, if there are team members absent, we can't cross train, so we can't become more flexible."

Team members need to understand that supporting the workforce becoming more flexible is part of why they come to work beyond just doing their jobs. No one is punished for staying home with the flu, but if they have perfect attendance, the organization will celebrate that.

This also begins to promote a healthy workforce with vaccines, wellness programs, and other ways to keep people healthy at home and at work. Now, people are rewarded for coming to work every day, becoming more multifunctional, and helping reach balanced scorecard targets. Everyone shares the same goal, and there is mutual trust and respect.

## *Celebrating Perfect Attendance*

The goal of perfect attendance is to celebrate behaviors. Whereas many organizations have point systems to track absenteeism and tardiness (the negative behaviors), the purpose of the perfect attendance system is to focus on the positive. Of course, a perfect attendance system alone won't work without the rest of the system. If the culture isn't in place—daily meetings, a suggestion system, leaders linked via the balanced scorecard—a perfect attendance system will not be effective. After Phase One is in place, the perfect attendance system will be very effective.

Perfect attendance is typically highlighted at the end of the year at a very nice rewards banquet to which spouses are also invited. There is usually additional compensation available to team members, leaders, and executives based on the policy/plan at this event. This way, when team members think they want to stay home "sick," their spouse reminds them that they want to attend the banquet and have an opportunity to win $10,000, a car, or whatever it may be. This is a great way to involve families, and the culture begins to spread throughout the community.

It's important to note that celebrating perfect attendance isn't just about the employees at the organization but also about their spouses. It should be a very nice celebration to say "Thank you." The celebration, if done correctly, can be the talk of the organization and even the talk of the town. It can be an event that spouses look forward to attending every year, encouraging them to help their spouses achieve perfect attendance.

As mentioned, this dinner includes classy entertainment and a gift giveaway—free dinners, tickets to sports games, gift certificates, and other prizes. At one organization, Rodger gave a car to one lucky employee with perfect attendance. The dinner was a five-star meal catered by the executives, who joined team members in the meal to celebrate the positive.

### *A Note on Teamwork and Perfect Attendance*

At one organization, a very upset union president took Rodger to see the pilot hall where a team had made an improvement.

This team had a board with pictures and names of all the team members to increase visual management and give executives the opportunity to match a face with a name to support the suggestion system, but an "absentee" block on the board visually highlighted which team members were absent yesterday and today.

The union leader feared this was an attempt to shame employees and pressure them to come to work, and he made it very clear that he wasn't going to tolerate this "improvement" or the embarrassment of a team member.

Rodger insisted that the union leader, Mark, speak with the team to understand the situation. During a break, Mark asked, "Why is John's picture up in the absentee block?"

A team member responded, "It's simple, Mark. When he comes back to work, we can observe and see if there's anything we can do to help him. For example, maybe there's an easier job we can put him on. If he's not feeling well, we might put him on a job where he'll be less likely to get injured. It's to help us help him."

In this example, the union president also happened to be the person responsible for the problem solving one standard training material at the company, and he learned his lesson. He stated that he should have used the 3Ps and 3Gs before jumping into action. It was a great lesson for everyone on the impact the system has on teamwork.

## Meeting Facilitation

Once Level A is working with daily problem solving, balanced scorecards, and the other tools, expectations become higher. Because people expect more from each other, tensions also increase. If the sensei isn't able to coach meeting facilitation and effective listening, conflicts will arise, and mutual trust/respect will be violated.

Effective communication helps people learn to listen and grasp necessary countermeasures from fragmented information. Later, meeting facilitation links with the five- minute rule, which is also introduced in Level C and discussed further below.

Meeting facilitation consists of a standardized approach to meetings—when to call them, publishing an agenda in advance, standards for documenting notes, and mechanisms for following up.

When the system is mature, or at least advanced in Level C, no one will want to go to a meeting where 27 pieces of paper are discussed yet yield little information. They will see the waste in meetings where problems are discussed that should be visualized and checked on a balanced scoreboard with teams that actively impact the countermeasures.

In Level C, meetings occur less frequently because leaders spend more time going and seeing, recognizing the positive, coaching improvements, and checking one-page reports. At leadership style meetings, leaders should come to their one-ups with two pieces of paper—a one-page report and a master plan.

When pilots start monthly meeting cycles, executives must grasp that they can't be at every meeting. The one-page report helps leaders perform PDCA in all areas, confirming how they can help. Meetings become more clearly linked to the balanced scorecard and specific improvement activities, and they must be effective or people will lose trust in the organization.

Conflict will arise for several positive reasons, but it must be managed proactively with meeting facilitation. First, the compensation structure should be linked to the balanced scorecard. If a metric's leader isn't achieving the metric, the team must help, but many will not know how best to offer support while advancing mutual trust and respect.

Second, it will no longer be possible for one team to have a green balanced scorecard while the supporting team has a red balanced scorecard because they are linked and impact each other.

Teaching meeting facilitation is necessary to manage focused improvement, i.e., group problem solving, kaizen events, and eventually quality control circles. These techniques help resolve conflict proactively and keep the team focused on positive behaviors and achieving the balanced scorecard results.

## Meeting Facilitation and Continuous Improvement (Kaizen) Events

Generally, meeting facilitation is introduced around the same time that kaizen events are introduced to advance the Continuous Improvement Program. People are solving more complex problems and are more prepared going into meetings, and they must have a standard for how to lead meetings effectively and plan follow-up activities.

Yes, kaizen events may use more advanced tools such as process mapping, value stream mapping, Fishbone diagrams, and other tools, but this is a natural progression of the tools. The 5 Whys will be ingrained in employees' thinking, and everyone will know the targets and the organization's true north. A kaizen event is really nothing more than team problem solving or team suggestions, with more advanced tools to support it, and most importantly the rest of the system in place to back it up.

During a kaizen event, different people have different roles. These may include the team leader, supervisor, and team members to support the problem(s) at hand. Meeting facilitation must be in place to help designate who gathers what information prior to the meeting. Meeting facilitation also helps designate how the meeting will be run as well as potential problems and proactive measures to avoid them. For the follow-up, meeting facilitation helps designate who will do what and when as well as which fourth row metrics need to be in place to check the actions during daily checks. The kaizen events and their team leaders are built in to the overall budget and staffing plan. Meeting facilitation is not used to schedule team members; it's used to determine how to solve problems as effectively and efficiently as possible.

As meetings become more effective and are planned proactively, vice presidents will lead quality circles that may span several months or a year. Meetings occur on schedule with a master plan, linked to hoshin, with specific checkpoints, and the leader must be very specific on the objectives for each meeting and the method necessary to achieve those objectives and results, staying on track with the master plan.

If the sensei doesn't teach meeting facilitation, there will be conflict because executives and other leaders won't achieve the scorecard, won't be on track with their master plans, and people's bonuses will be affected. The skills of meeting facilitation are very important and are sharpened as the Continuous Improvement Program evolves.

### Effective Listening

In Level C, leaders get much more information through go and sees, informal conversations, daily meetings, one-page reports, and other sources. They must grasp how to take that fragmented information and comprehend the situation and relate it to the business case and the leadership framework.

Effective listening is about hearing the right information without reading a 20-page report 30 days later, because no one has time for that. Listening effectively using daily or hourly checks means leaders can grasp the situation and solve problems in the moment while sustaining previous improvements.

Learning to hear and listen is like learning to see. It doesn't come naturally, and it's a progression for leaders. Learning to hear and listen is completely different from listening in a conversation. It's about hearing fragmented information and linking it to visual information to draw the most appropriate conclusions very quickly.

Everyone needs to be taught effective listening skills, and meeting facilitation and conflict resolution help do this. Without these skills, many leaders hear what they want to hear, not what others want them to hear, and not what they need to hear to improve the process and develop people.

For example, if sent to meet with a supplier, those with an effective listening mindset will hear things they've never heard before and can help the supplier relationship by solving problems. In world-class organizations, time is of the essence, and effective listening is critical to understanding things quickly.

## Five-Minute Rule

As the system matures, it's critical that leaders comprehend problem solving, one-page reports, standard work, balanced scorecards, and other artifacts of TPS in a short period of time to support real-time decision making and problem solving.

The five-minute rule has many applications, but it essentially means that everything (problem, solution, etc.) needs to be understandable within five minutes or there's something wrong with the standard. If a problem can't be communicated in five minutes, the standardization hasn't been done adequately. If a one-page report or balanced scorecard isn't clear on what the action or the go and see needs to be within five minutes, it's not as effective as it needs to be.

It's surprising how many organizations are considered world class, yet when leaders walk around the company, they can't explain a chart, the standard, or a visual tool to support the process.

At Toyota and other truly world-class companies, team members can do the 5 Whys mentally and immediately begin implementing countermeasures. This isn't because team members are smarter or because andons call leaders to the line to help solve the problem fast; it's because the standards are so clear that anyone can comprehend the problem, take it to its source, and implement countermeasures quickly.

Without the five-minute rule, it becomes very difficult for anyone to solve problems quickly and expect them to stay solved. Without Levels A and B in place, it's very difficult to do root cause analysis quickly, visualize what's necessary on the balanced scorecard, and apply simple countermeasures.

## Introduction to Total Preventative Maintenance (TPM)

Most people understand total preventative maintenance as "cleaning machines so they don't break down." That's very obvious and it must be done, but total preventative maintenance within TPS is much, much deeper than merely "cleaning machines."

Total preventative maintenance includes basic things that keep and maintain processes without the support of external departments as well as total preventative maintenance of the entire system. True total preventative maintenance integrates maintaining man, machine, material, and method as much as possible without calling someone else for support. From a global perspective, total preventative maintenance aims to maintain the system, i.e., the gains that have already been made via the Transformation Curve.

### Total Preventative Maintenance of Machines and Process

At a basic level, how do secretaries maintain phones, computers, copy machines, and office equipment? If information services are tied up firefighting, how can they manage problems proactively and think strategically?

On the shop floor, how do frontline team members maintain their processes, inputs, and outputs? What can they do to contribute? What are their checks of the process and the system? What can they control so that the process flows uninterrupted and they don't have to pull the andon for simple, preventable problems? What can they control without having a negative impact on the balanced scorecard?

This doesn't mean working outside of one's scope, like a nurse performing surgery or a line worker messing with an electrical box, but can the nurse maintain surgical instruments in the operating room without calling biomedical engineering? Can the line worker change a light bulb without calling an electrician or maintenance?

Total preventative maintenance creates a multifunctional workforce that has the responsibility and authority to both control the process and make improvements.

*Total Preventative Maintenance of the System*

How are Levels A, B, and C maintained?

New employees must all be trained on Level A and exhibit its behaviors—balanced scorecard, safety system, suggestion system, problem solving one, and other tools—in order to maintain the gains.

From a global standpoint, continuous improvement team members must never lose their Level A skills. If individuals don't practice the 5 Whys and start looking for big wins, the organization will be out of balance. The culture will disappear, everybody will be doing kaizen events without daily problem solving and suggestions, and 90% of the problems won't be solved.

Without total preventative maintenance of the system, the basic things that changed the culture and moved the organization to where it is today will fall by the wayside.

This is where annual planning is very important.

If a PDCA cycle in the system isn't tightened up at least daily and the systematic approach can't be maintained, including the balanced scorecard, problem solving, 5S, kanbans, andons, roles/responsibilities, standard work, management cycle, and other tools, total preventative maintenance isn't working as intended.

The higher you go in the organization, the more the system is looked at holistically. In maturity audits, the continuous improvement team should be asking, "Are we really maintaining the system?" At the same time, executives may be concerned with, "Am I developing my leaders for succession in five or ten years?"

It's easy to introduce the tools systematically compared to maintaining them and developing leaders. Often, sustaining them is very difficult, because the organization has seen improvement and thinks, "Since there's improvement, that's good enough."

At one organization, Phase One was in place but wasn't being maintained. After a few years, the company still hadn't advanced into the rest of the Transformation Curve, including total preventative maintenance. Though executives patted themselves on the backs and talked about problems, they avoided using problem-solving sheets.

Total preventative maintenance and maturity audit one help to maintain and identify problems within the system, but if basic problem solving isn't working, if there's no system to link top problems with the suggestion system, it's very easy for the organization to backslide and lose momentum. Total preventative maintenance helps ensure the system in place is working as it should be.

Most people who say they understand Lean or know Toyota define total preventative maintenance from a maintenance/machine standpoint and don't grasp that the audits and total preventative maintenance are linked and maintain the system. Leaders must identify when the organization is losing basic skills like the 5 Whys and 5S and maintain behaviors via total preventative maintenance, checking them off via maturity audits one, two, and three.

That's why the audit comes before total preventative maintenance. If there's no mechanism in place, maintenance will be overlooked and/or won't be effective. If total preventative maintenance isn't done, behaviors start to collapse. Once this happens, they drag the system down with them.

## The Goal—Overlapping Level C with the Journey to World Class

To fully learn and adapt the Transformation Curve, it's important to remember the concept of first things first. Phase One must be in place before a perfect attendance program is implemented. If people aren't engaged in the Continuous Improvement Program, if they can't see how their behaviors impact results and link to the strategy, this program may not be successful and may have many unintended consequences. Generally, any tool implemented in isolation from the rest of the system will fail or be unsustainable.

Each tool of Level C must be grasped from the executive level, from a policy standpoint, and from an actual doing standpoint. Then, leaders must be engaged in understanding and establishing policies to support the tools. Organizations that rush to one-page reports without the daily key performance indicators, the daily behaviors, and the detail to support one-page reports might find success, but it generally won't be linked to a long-term strategy.

Likewise, executives must use one-page reports to check and summarize top-level master plans, top-level balanced scorecards, the status of the continuous improvement program, and the status of the pilot hall. Linking one-page reports from the executive team and the pilot area helps to create alignment and increases go and sees at the right place at the right time.

The tools of the Transformation Curve are introduced in sequence for a reason, with later tools building upon earlier ones. Without a systematic approach to introduce and build upon earlier knowledge, organizations may just use tools to solve problems and develop people. This may result in improvement but only of a limited nature.

On the other hand, using the Transformation Curve and understanding the basic steps of the journey allows organizations to move towards world-class performance.

www.ingramcontent.com/pod-product-compliance
Lightning Source LLC
Chambersburg PA
CBHW020426010526
44118CB00010B/450